Lifelong Learning in the UK

Written specifically for Education Studies students, this accessible text offers a clear introduction to lifelong learning and the impact it has on all areas of society. Assuming no prior knowledge of the subject, it explores what lifelong learning is, where learning can and does take place and who is accessing it.

Offering a clear overview of the different strands to lifelong learning, the book examines the concept, drawing on key policy initiatives and strategies. Each section outlines the types of individuals who are most likely to access lifelong learning within and across these strands including migrants, refugees and asylum seekers, unemployed adults, carers and guardians, older age-groups and returning learners.

Chapters cover:

- adult and community learning;
- higher education;
- further education;
- work-based learning;
- prison and probation learning.

Including supporting tasks and reflection activities, this textbook will give students a broad understanding of lifelong learning and its role in supporting adults throughout their life both socially and economically. *Lifelong Learning in the UK* is an essential introductory text for students on undergraduate courses in Education Studies.

Anne O'Grady is Senior Lecturer in Education Studies at the University of Derby, UK.

Lifelong Learning in the UK

An introductory guide for Education Studies

Anne O'Grady

 Routledge
Taylor & Francis Group

LONDON AND NEW YORK

First published 2013
by Routledge
2 Park Square, Milton Park, Abingdon, Oxon OX14 4RN

Simultaneously published in the USA and Canada
by Routledge
711 Third Avenue, New York, NY 10017

Routledge is an imprint of the Taylor & Francis Group, an informa business

British Library Cataloguing in Publication Data
A catalogue record for this book is available from the British Library

Library of Congress Cataloging in Publication Data
O'Grady, Anne (Educator), author.
  Lifelong learning in the UK : an introductory guide for education studies /
  Anne O'Grady.
    pages cm
  1. Continuing education – Great Britain.   2. Adult education – Great
  Britain.   I. Title.
  LC5256.G7O37 2013+
  374′.941 – dc23
                                                        2012045694

ISBN: 978-0-415-51741-6 (hbk)
ISBN: 978-0-415-51742-3 (pbk)
ISBN: 978-0-203-12371-3 (ebk)

Typeset in Bembo
by RefineCatch Limited, Bungay, Suffolk

MIX
Paper from
responsible sources
FSC   FSC® C013056
www.fsc.org

Printed and bound in Great Britain by
TJ International Ltd, Padstow, Cornwall

10/2/13

Contents

Preface

'Lifelong learning' is a term that is now widely adopted and used by all sectors of society to describe a learning experience. However, it is a very slippery concept which changes and evolves over time, with different political parties giving it different meaning and weighting, demonstrated largely in the form of financial resources and backing.

During the most recent New Labour government (and historic Labour governments) lifelong learning has benefited from substantial investments, strategies and policies to try to develop a cultural acceptance, tolerance and adoption of lifelong learning as part of a 'natural order of things' within society. This can be seen, for example, in strategies such as *Skills for Life* (DfEE, 2001a) and the higher education *Widening Participation Strategy* (DfES, 2003e).

The Conservative approach to embracing lifelong learning has been more conservative – with a little 'c' – often resulting in a 'rolling back' of centralised action, preferring instead to adopt a much more market-led approach, seen for example in the 1992 *Further and Higher Education Act* (Great Britain, 1992) which introduced the idea of student tuition fees.

The ambitions and plans for lifelong learning in England, currently being formed and forged by the Coalition Liberal Democrat–Conservative government are now becoming clear, as can be seen for example in the *Skills for Sustainable Growth* (DBIS, 2010b) strategy, *The Browne Report* (Browne, 2010) and *The Wolf Report* (Wolf, 2011). These documents reveal a very different perspective on the role, purpose and meaning of lifelong learning for contemporary England over the next decade.

This book aims to introduce you to the concept of lifelong learning, reflecting on its historical growth in order to situate it in contemporary thinking and practice, and then offer a debate on the meaning of lifelong learning for the contemporary UK going forward.

This book is intended primarily for students who are studying Education Studies in the UK, and are interested in understanding education from a range of perspectives, and particularly for thinking about the areas where learning happens beyond the parameters of traditional compulsory education.

As Education Studies students, it is reasonable to assume that you are interested in the concept of education – where it happens, how it happens, and perhaps more importantly, why does it happen and to whom. This book aims to introduce you to an arena of education that sits on the periphery of modern-day constructs of education that, arguably, position education in a linear fashion that starts formally and ends formally, with most people starting at the primary level of education and finishing at secondary levels.

It – lifelong learning – is a very messy, chaotic and diverse sector that provides a whole range of learning opportunities for our society. The umbrella term for the sector is the lifelong learning sector, but the terminology associated with the sector changes and evolves regularly – often linked to new political landscapes and political change. The changing nature of the terminology used to describe the sector can lead to confusion or misunderstanding. Throughout the following chapters, the various strands of the lifelong learning sector will be introduced, described and discussed. The key policies that have influenced the sector will be outlined, and the stakeholders involved in delivering the services will be introduced. Importantly, the learners – those who are supported in their engagement with the provision – will be highlighted. However, it is important to recognise that I have made these delineations for the purpose of writing, and that the system is not always as clear cut as this book might imply. Lifelong learning happens in a range of guises, in a multitude of places, and in a multitude of ways – that's what makes it both exciting and frustrating!

Wherever, and in whatever capacity, Education Studies graduates find themselves following graduation, the need for continued engagement in learning will be apparent – personally or professionally. Students need to be aware of the broad remit that is covered by lifelong learning, including: formal and informal types of learning; where learning can and does take place; who is accessing it; and importantly how and why it is accessed. Students of Education Studies should be critically aware of the role of lifelong learning in the contemporary UK and should be able to discuss, evaluate and analyse the benefits of lifelong learning in all areas of society – politically, economically and socially. This book aims to assist you in this task.

Chapter 1 introduces you to the concept of lifelong learning and discusses the emergence of this concept and its relevance and importance for contemporary UK society. It considers some of the key terms associated with lifelong learning, and explores the various definitions developed to explain the concept.

Chapter 2 then moves on to explore what lifelong learning means in practice, and introduces some of the key policies that have informed the framework for the delivery of lifelong learning in contemporary UK society. The chapter considers who is involved in lifelong learning; the curriculum offer of lifelong learning; where lifelong learning takes place; and who facilitates lifelong learning programmes.

Chapter 3 focuses on lifelong learning from the perspective of adult and community learning. It will consider the concept of 'community' and explore lifelong learning for social benefits, and wider benefits beyond economic outcomes. The chapter will explore where such lifelong learning opportunities occur in the community and whether they have at their heart a particular community agenda. The chapter highlights particular types of lifelong learning, including family learning; learning for those not in education employment or training (NEETs); learning for marginalised groups, such as gang members or those engaged in substance misuse and abuse; lifelong learning programmes for health and wellbeing; learning for migrant communities; and learning for older people and those who live in rural communities. The chapter highlights some of the key stakeholders involved in supporting adult and community lifelong learning and considers how such learning is funded.

Chapter 4 introduces lifelong learning and higher education, discussing particularly the contribution of higher education to the lifelong learning offer in contemporary UK society through the widening participation agenda. The chapter firstly maps out the historical rise of widening participation strategies across the UK before going on to question how our society has established mechanisms to maintain social structures, particularly through the higher education framework. The chapter considers how we can work towards progression and development that enables the creation of a more equal society through widening participation strategies, by exploring key concepts including social, economic and cultural capital, as well as social mobility.

Chapter 5 explores lifelong learning within the context of further education. As perhaps the most significant and well-known strand of the lifelong learning sector, this chapter questions the contribution of further education to lifelong learning in contemporary UK society. The chapter considers the range of learning opportunities provided through further education and explores the challenges they face as they are driven forward by new policy frameworks resulting from the election of the Coalition Liberal Democrat–Conservative government in May 2010.

Chapter 6 introduces lifelong learning that occurs through work-based learning, starting at the point of pre-employment. The chapter considers the concepts of unemployment, employment and employability, before considering the lifelong learning opportunities for the unemployed. The chapter then moves on to consider the range of lifelong learning opportunities within the workplace, including continuous professional development. The key stakeholders and organisations supporting work-based lifelong learning are highlighted. The chapter concludes with an introduction to the new apprenticeship framework, which sits at the heart of the new Coalition ambition for the development of lifelong learning in contemporary UK society.

Chapter 7 introduces you to the final strand of the lifelong learning sector in contemporary UK society – lifelong learning for offenders. The chapter explores the reasons that underpin lifelong learning in prison environments, through the current lifelong learning policy framework; the key stakeholders and agencies involved in providing and supporting lifelong learning; and questions whether prison environments should support such an offer.

Chapter 8 concludes the book, and considers the challenges and opportunities for lifelong learning in the context of the future of contemporary UK society, and ambitiously attempts to locate UK lifelong learning within a global framework.

Throughout the book you will find a range of supporting Tasks and Reflection activities. These have been positioned throughout the book to enable you to spend some time thinking more deeply about the area of discussion, to seek out further source information, or to enable you to reinforce and confirm your understanding of the topic under discussion. These activities are designed to enable you to think critically both about the sector of lifelong learning – from the perspective of policy-makers who, arguably, drive the sector through funding and resource provision, and from the perspective of the learner and their demands and needs from the system. You are encouraged to engage with these tasks to deepen your understanding of lifelong learning in contemporary UK society.

The ambition of this book is raise the profile of lifelong learning in contemporary UK society, and enable you to acknowledge and critically reflect on your role within the sector, as emergent Education Studies graduates. By the end of the book, it is expected that you will be able to demonstrate a growing knowledge of the sector and its role in contemporary society – socially and economically. It is also hoped that you will develop an understanding of how learning occurs in a variety of ways, with many different purposes – it is more than just the acquisition of qualifications for the purposes of economic benefit, although that is a very real and important aspect of lifelong learning provision.

1

Introduction to lifelong learning

Introduction

Lifelong learning has been variously considered over the decades as the key to the development of a society that is economically successful within a global market, but that is also inclusive and just (Hodgson and Spours, 1999). Lifelong learning has been discussed within a framework of emancipation and oppression (Freire, 1996) and has often been portrayed as the key to survival; as the foundation of learning organisations, a learning society and a learning culture (Kerka, 2000; Field, 2002). More recent discussions regarding lifelong learning have identified it as a concept that has at its core the notion that learning takes place throughout one's life (Schuller and Watson, 2009).

This chapter will introduce the concept of lifelong learning. It will discuss the emergence of this concept and its relevance and importance for society today.

To aid the flow of discussion, the chapter sets out a series of questions. It is important to note that I do no expect to be able to answer these questions fully, but to draw on my experiences, reading of the literature and research to assist in the development of answers to these questions. I say this because often as a student, when you read an academic text, it is not uncommon to make some assumptions that the academic community has all the answers and that what is written is the 'truth'. You are invited during the course of this book to question what is written, challenge the response, and perhaps most importantly think about what is missing. For example, in writing my responses what have I chosen not to write?

The key question for this chapter is: what is 'lifelong learning'? In developing a response to this question I will explore some of the key terms often drawn on to inform thinking about the subject, and which may create contradictions or ambiguity. By then end of the chapter you should be able to develop a definition of lifelong learning. You should begin to be able to understand the challenges and difficulties associated with developing this definition which will, in turn, inform your reading throughout the text.

Task

Attempt to write a definition of lifelong learning. You will be able to reflect, and build on this definition as you engage with this text.

What is 'lifelong learning'?

Defining terms

Lifelong learning, as a concept, should not be as difficult to understand as it seems. While it should be acknowledged that lifelong learning happens in a variety of places, in a variety of ways, and engages with all sectors of society – and so is not as 'neat' as the compulsory sector of education – extra layers of ambiguity are developed by the changing nature of the terminology that is used to describe or discuss lifelong learning. Some common terms used by the sector and throughout the literature around lifelong learning include: *post-compulsory education, vocational education, continuing education, adult education, lifelong education, learning through the life-course* and *continuing professional development*. For the purpose of this text the term lifelong learning will be used to explore this sector of learning.

In discussions around lifelong learning, multiple terms are used, often interchangeably, in the same text as well as across texts. In order to develop a clear understanding of lifelong learning, you should be able to distinguish the different underlying meanings of each of these associated key terms, particularly 'adult', 'education' and 'training', 'globalisation', 'skills' and 'lifelong learning'.

In order to understand lifelong learning, it is important to be able to distinguish it from other terms that have been used across the decades to explain learning that occurs outside of the compulsory education framework in the UK. The following section invites you to think about some common everyday terms that we use in society unquestioningly, and asks you to query them and develop your own understanding of the terms and what they might mean within the context of lifelong learning. By doing this you should develop a stronger understanding of what lifelong learning might mean for you.

Adult

The term 'adult' is one that we use every day without any particular thought. However, it is essential for us to understand who we are referring to when we talk about an 'adult'. Often we think about being an adult as reaching a particular age, and legally in the UK you become an adult at the age of 18. However, many lifelong learning funding streams consider 'adult' as 19 and often 25 for 'mature learners', or indeed 24 for learners with learning difficulties and disabilities.

Rogers (2003) provides a very broad and helpful discussion on the notion of 'adult'. In his argument, he identifies that the term 'adult' has been, and continues to be, used in a number of ways. Often 'adult' is associated with chronological age, but to be 'adult' is also associated with particular attitudes, values and beliefs, and linked to certain types of behaviour. 'Adult' or 'adulthood' is often rooted to a cultural specificity, and can be seen as a social construct that holds particular meaning and perception for specific cultures. Examples of a range of definitions for what it means to be an adult can be identified in the literature, ranging from an adult 'defined as anyone aged twenty-one or over, married, or the head of a household' (Johnstone and Rivera in Rogers, 2003: 26) to people defined as 'adults because they have assumed responsibility for managing their own lives' (Merriam and Caffarella in Rogers, 2003: 393). Rogers asserts that adulthood, in Western societies, is seen as the opposite of childhood and that 'adultness' can be identified by three signifying characteristics: maturity, autonomy and a sense of perspective in relation to self.

Importantly, notions of adulthood, and what it means to be adult, are fluid and ever changing. Individuals construct their own conceptions of what it is to be adult based on their own contexts of culture and society. Throughout this book 'adult' is used as a chronological reference to people aged between 19 and 65 and associated with paid employment, rather than as a concept with associated value and belief systems, although these are implicit. When thinking about 'young people', this will refer to those people between the ages of 14 and 19 who form a significant part of the lifelong learning sector.

Education and training within lifelong learning

In the UK, compulsory education has been in place since the nineteenth century. While it has undergone many changes and developments, fundamentally children and young people are required to engage in formal learning processes identified by the government from the ages of approximately 5 to 16. Forms of compulsory education are explored in detail in other texts and will not be discussed here. However, it is important to note that the term 'education' has been widely used in discussions around learning beyond compulsory education and it is important to be clear about what 'education' means in the context of learning, as this can significantly inform and influence how we think about lifelong learning.

Education

'Education' is a term that is frequently interchanged with the term 'training'. However, these terms have very different meanings which are particularly important when thinking about what constitutes lifelong learning. Education is often regarded, and commonly thought about, as:

> organised and sustained instruction designed to communicate a combination of knowledge, skills and understanding valuable for all the activities of life.
>
> (Jarvis, 1987: 105)

Education, according to Raymond Williams, is underpinned by a series of philosophical ambitions: to enable individuals to understand social change; to enable them to relate social change to their own context; and to enable individuals to become the authors of social change. This framework for education provides a good platform for thinking about what lifelong learning is, and supports the work of influential writers in the world of lifelong learning such as Dewey (1916), as well as people such as Knowles (1975) and Jarvis (1987, 1995, 2006, 2007, 2011) amongst others. These thinkers based their philosophy of learning on a humanistic model which will be explored further in this chapter.

Task

Take a moment here to think about your own experience of education and what education means for you. What do you think you learnt as you went through your education? What was the purpose of your education and who decided what should or should not be taught? Was it, for example, to be economically successful, or was it so that you learnt the appropriate way to behave in society? Perhaps you think it was so that you could influence your own engagement with society or others.

Training

The term 'training' can be used to denote something different to the term 'education', and is generally considered to be an activity which involves the transfer of knowledge and skills from an 'expert' or 'professional' to a 'new student or employee' in order that the student becomes enabled to undertake the newly learned skill independently. This is usually experienced within an economic environment or a workplace (Jarvis, 1995).

There is extensive debate and tension around, and between, the terms education and training, with a value hierarchy associated with them being evidenced in discussions around curriculum models (Jarvis, 1995); often described as the academic–vocational divide. An academic curriculum largely incorporates material that may be deemed to be important in its own right without any real concern about whether the material can or should be useful for economic activity. Such a curriculum is likely to incorporate elements of cultural heritage, with associated political and cultural value-judgements. Alternatively, a vocational curriculum predominantly incorporates only materials that are based on what participants will need to know in order to carry out a particular activity, job or role; the use of the new material is given more importance than the knowledge of the material. Academic learning, or education, is most often privileged over training or vocational learning (Armitage et al., 2003).

Coffield (1997) highlights the difficultly of interchangeably using the terms 'learning' and 'education'. He argues that when the word 'learning' is used, particularly in policy documents, as part of the term 'lifelong learning', the intended or implied meaning is 'planned, purposeful and intended learning' which is more closely associated with 'education'; rather than the type of learning people engage in all the time – the ongoing process of change and adaptation to life circumstances, which may more closely align with lifelong learning. This is what Rogers (2004) refers to as informal learning, and is arguably most closely associated with original perspectives on the purpose and role of lifelong learning.

What is apparent is that education is a politically driven instrument that fundamentally influences the ways in which society both exists and evolves. Education generally has a clear curriculum outline which leads to the opportunity to demonstrate that learning has been achieved through qualification – the model of education in the UK. While some elements exist within lifelong learning discourse, the learning opportunities encapsulated in the concept of lifelong learning are much broader than this narrow perspective of learning.

Globalisation and a knowledge economy

It is important to recognise the role of lifelong learning in the UK within a global framework. 'Globalisation' is an umbrella term used to explain increasing global connectivity, integration and interdependence in a range of spheres, particularly economic activity, and has become increasingly popular during the twentieth century as a way of explaining the relationships that exist to bind people into one global system of activity. The rapid growth in globalisation is largely identified through three primary areas of activity: economic, social and political, resulting in a 'global economy'.

The role of lifelong learning as a tool for both economic prosperity and social responsibility is widely acknowledged by governments across the world. The emergence of lifelong learning as part of a 'knowledge-based economy' (Drucker, 2003) refers to the use of knowledge to produce economic benefit. Drucker (2003) described economic globalisation in terms of 'transition' – moving towards a 'knowledge economy' or 'information society'. The rise of globalisation, and the associated knowledge-based economy, has resulted in the development of goods and services that can be bought, sold and delivered, and as such globalisation demands 'a more educated and continually educated, workforce' (Jarvis, 2007: 63) – arguably, a lifelong approach to learning that, importantly, is seen as the responsibility of the individual, not just the state.

Globalisation and lifelong learning

Lifelong learning has gained increasing prominence. During the 1970s influential debates on the role of lifelong learning were undertaken by the United Nations Educational, Scientific and Cultural Organization (UNESCO, online), resulting in the publication of the Faure report in 1972 (Faure et al., 1972). This report continued to support a largely humanistic view of learning, recognising formal, non-formal and informal learning for all people throughout their lifetime.

The Organisation for Economic Co-operation and Development's (OECD) approach to lifelong learning, however, went on to develop a much more human-capital (economic) view of lifelong learning, conceptualising lifelong learning as 'recurrent education' (OECD, 1973) that enabled individuals to experience phases of paid work, leisure and learning. In Britain, the Russell Committee was appointed to advise Government on adult education policies and to support the creation of a number of lifelong learning pathways, including the provision of basic literacy teaching (DES, 1973).

As a result of the changing nature of the global economic market, 'lifelong learning as a concept became rooted on an economy of full employment' (Field, 2001: 8).

However, the association of lifelong learning with economic outcomes is open to criticism (see, for example, Coffield, 1999), particularly around turning education from a 'public good' into a private commodity. By shifting responsibility for learning to the individual, Coffield argued that the socially constructed nature of learning becomes ignored and instrumental and vocational learning becomes overemphasised, with only those activities that show a visible and quick return being rewarded (Coffield, 1999). This is an important area of argument and debate in relation to the purpose and function of lifelong learning and one you are encouraged to review and reflect on as you analyse the concept of lifelong learning throughout the course of this book.

Following the work of UNESCO and the OCED, the European Year of Lifelong Learning was established in 1996 and lifelong learning became a central part of national policy debates. It has continued to play its part in legitimating a wide range of policy activity. Field (2001: 3–4) argued that lifelong learning has increasingly become 'a tool for the reform and modernisation of aspects of national education and training systems' and consequently 'is likely to become one among many factors that are transforming the governance of late modern societies'. Writing a decade later, it is interesting to note both the continued and heightened political engagement in lifelong learning and its role in economic and social activity in the UK.

Perspectives and interpretations of 'learning'

The concept of lifelong learning is complicated by the interchangeable use by writers of the terms lifelong 'learning' and lifelong 'education' (Rogers, 1992, 2002, 2004), and also by how 'learning' is regarded and defined. These discussions are premised on a philosophical perspective and view (or theory) of learning, and are often discussed as 'schools' of thought. A very brief outline of these various perspectives are provided here to aid understanding of lifelong learning, but you are encouraged to read more widely to develop broader understanding of these various philosophical perspectives of the notion of learning.

These philosophical positions can be broken down into four distinct schools of thought. Firstly, the *behaviourist approach* contends that all learning involves observable changes in behaviour. Key writers in this school include Pavlov and his stimulus–response model of learning, Skinner's operant conditioning model of learning and Thorndike's law of effect (see Armitage, et al., 2003 for a brief introduction).

A second perspective is the *gestalt branch*, founded in the 1920s by Wertheimer, Kohler and Koffka (see Jarvis, 1995). This approach focuses on the mind's perceptive process and is based on the idea of whole structures and patterns. This approach considers learning as a complex process of interrelationships that occur as a result of engaging with new problems in the light of previous experiences (Jarvis, 1995).

Thirdly, the cognitive branch of learning theory is based on the work of Piaget and Bruner who determined that knowledge was constructed through interactions with the environment, with learning occurring through experimentation and discovery: termed *constructivism*. Piaget's research focused on the development of children and established that learning was developmental, and went on to identify stages of sequential intellectual development. Bruner's work followed on from Piaget's, stating that discovery learning was the most effective and authentic method of achieving a real understanding of the principles of a subject (Jarvis, 1995).

The fourth philosophical approach to learning is a *humanist* approach that places emphasis on a perceived 'natural desire' of all humans to learn, maintaining that learners need to be empowered and have control over the learning process. Theorists in this perspective include Dewey, Rogers and Knowles. Knowles was largely responsible for the popularisation of the term 'andragogy' – the art and science of helping adults to learn, based on a notion of adults as self-directed learners. Rogers also placed emphasis on the self, and contended that learning was acquired by doing and therefore experiential learning can be the only true learning that exists (Illeris, 2004).

These differing theoretical approaches to learning provide contrasting claims about the effectiveness of learning, and about the relationship between learning and knowledge, and should be (and are) contested. What can be observed from these varying perspectives on learning is that 'learning' occurs in a diverse set of ways. However, what constitutes learning is very often associated with formal models of education, and hence the interchangeable nature of the terms 'learning' and 'education' can be explained. The term 'education' can be identified as a process through which learning can be facilitated, while other forms of learning, such as non-formal (learning outside a formal learning system) and informal (learning from life), are considered within a lifelong learning framework to be of equal value to that undertaken through more formal pathways (traditionally teacher-centred and facilitated environments) (Rogers, 2004).

Reflection

How do you think each of these approaches to learning can inform a definition of lifelong learning?

Formal, non-formal and informal lifelong learning

Above is outlined the theoretical positioning of what constitutes learning. In contemporary UK society, however, learning is often explained in terms of outcomes – learning that leads to some form of tangible outcome, most commonly qualifications, which are further subdivided by levels. Non-formal or informal learning, however, can be associated with either incidental learning that happens as part of ones existence and is generally not facilitated – for example knowing when to speak or when to listen in a conversation – or can be used to describe learning which is facilitated but is not necessarily associated with a qualification, for example leisure classes, art classes or political groups.

All types of learning are given value across the lifelong learning sector. Rogers (2004) provides a useful critique of the different types of learning and the value placed on each type of learning activity by members of our society. Qualification-driven learning is most often highly valued in society because it provides external confirmation of one's ability to learn at a particular level, and it provides some 'currency' that is valued in the employment market – probably two of the key reasons why you are studying for a degree. However, while this is commendable, our challenge as a society is to recognise and value all types of learning – whether that is learning to develop an awareness or understanding of art, music or each other. The value of learning for social justice, I would suggest, is one to strive for and can be achieved through a better understanding of lifelong learning. A more focused and targeted development of lifelong learning policy would usefully contribute to both the economic and social ambitions for the country set out by the new Coalition government.

Skills and lifelong learning

The concept of 'skills' in relation to discussions of lifelong learning is gathering momentum and can be seen particularly across policy discourse (see for example Leitch's *Review of Skills* (2006), *Skills for Sustainable Growth*, (DBIS, 2010b). The Labour party introduced the term during the first half of the millennium with Gordon Brown reframing one of their best-known election campaign slogans, 'education, education, education', as 'skills, skills, skills' and in doing so providing a clear demonstration and focus for the purpose and role of lifelong learning in the contemporary UK.

The policy discussion in the following chapter outlines how this shift in terminology has influenced the lifelong learning sector. The Coalition party have adapted this term and drawn on it heavily to provide a message of focus for lifelong learning during the second decade of this millennium, with the department responsible for the sector being the Department for Business, Innovation and Skills, and the sector being referred to as the further education and skills sector. 'Skills' now forms a major focus of (and for) lifelong learning, with many programmes and interventions being associated with 'skills development'.

The emergence of the concept of lifelong learning

Above, we have considered the concept of 'adult' and 'education' separately. Lifelong learning has long been associated with adult education, and indeed, in the literature, lifelong learning is a term that is used alongside terms such as 'adult education', 'lifelong education' or 'post-compulsory education' to refer to the same area of learning. I will refer to the construct as lifelong learning for the purposes of this text.

Lifelong learning as a concept has been present in Britain since at least the eighteenth century (Yeaxlee, 1929). It has largely remained on the perimeter of educational provision and has generally been associated with the socialisation of young people or remedial, or second chance, education for adults.

Lifelong learning has, at its core, the notion that learning takes place throughout one's life (Schuller and Watson, 2009). Adult education, or lifelong learning, in Britain has long been associated with an agenda of, and for, social change (Bynner and Parsons, 1998; DfEE, 1998; Bowman, et al., 2000; DfEE, 2001a). Participation in adult education has been identified as an important driver in affecting such change (Bynner and Parsons, 1998). This agenda has been further heightened during the last two decades, becoming a key government priority and a central indicator upon which success[1] is measured in education and in other areas, such as increased employment (DfEE, 1999; DfEE, 2001b; DfES, 2003a; DIUS, 2007; DBIS, 2010a).

The concept of lifelong learning has, in recent decades, also acquired global recognition, with 1996 being declared the European Year of Lifelong Learning by the

European Union, and has increasingly been portrayed by successive governments as the key to survival (Kerka, 2000; Field, 2002).

At its origins, lifelong learning was explored as the concept of *lifelong education*. Lifelong education emerged during the 1960s as a humanistic and radical approach to education with the aim of transforming both economic and social structures, such as capitalism, through an emphasis on informal[2] learning across one's lifespan (Freire, 1996).

Lifelong learning has experienced a political transformation from one that held a humanistic radical approach to education to one with a focus on economy, skills and vocationalism, and this transformation can be seen in the policy discourse associated with lifelong learning. Field argues that:

> By individualising the characteristics that justify employees and others in treating people differently, the trend towards lifelong learning also helps fragment the excluded, and encourages a search for individual solutions ... the most significant of which include training, so that individuals can acquire the skills and knowledge required for them to take active responsibility for their own well-being.
>
> (Field, 2001: 13–14)

While there continues to be a clear emphasis on the economic benefits associated with the concept of lifelong learning, there is a parallel discourse focusing on the development of sustainable communities through an agenda of social justice and a reduction in social exclusion.

By providing opportunities for lifelong learning, authors have continually argued that people will be better able to participate in, and take responsibility for, their communities (Freire, 1996; Street, 2004; OECD, 1996). However, as noted by Kerka (2000), dichotomies can be drawn between participants and non-participants, or learners and non-learners, which may work to increase the divide between 'those who can' and 'those who can't'.

Lifelong learning, then, is an eclectic concept that is broad and multifaceted; it is intertwined with other concepts such as lifelong education, continuing education and adult education. However, it is also apparent that a contemporary understanding of lifelong learning is closely linked to economic values that tend to override humanitarian aims. Lifelong learning has 'become a means of achieving instrumental (economic) values, an end in itself that would enhance personal development' (Lee, 2007: 1). It is most often associated with activities that aim to improve knowledge, skills and competence and has become a policy goal for supporting economic growth.

Lifelong learning: towards a definition

Defining lifelong learning is, arguably, impossible. Many key writers and authors over time (see for example Field, Jarvis, Rogers, Knowles, Schuller) have all provided some interesting critiques, debates and arguments about what lifelong learning is. Some are based on notions of 'capital' development (either economic or social), and some on continuous personal or professional development. What seems to be apparent is that lifelong learning has a dualism of economic and social effect associated with it, with some authors prioritising one aspect over the other. For example, while government policy documents over the last two decades or so have discussed the parallel benefits of engaging in lifelong learning for the individual and for society – for social well-being and economic prosperity – in reality funding streams demonstrate a stronger focus on economic returns for the individual and thereby the country. As you read through this introductory text, you should start to consider what lifelong learning means for you within the framework of contemporary education in the UK: do you value lifelong learning and in what ways?

The European Commission in 2001 suggested that lifelong learning could be considered as:

> all learning activity undertaken through life, with the aim of improving knowledge skills and competences within a personal, civic, social and/or employment-related perspective.
>
> (Jarvis, 2011: 9)

This is a reasonable definition of lifelong learning as a starting point from which to think about it.

In 2009, the National Institute of Adult Continuing Education (NIACE) published the results of their inquiry into the future for lifelong learning. The inquiry reports on a vision of learning through life for the future. When reporting their findings, Schuller and Watson (2009: 9), who led the inquiry, found an interpretation of 'lifelong' as referring to something that occurs from 'cradle to grave'. However, it is important to recognise that the main focus of the inquiry was on adult learning (see discussion above) and particularly on adults returning to learning, and therefore did not focus on learning that occurred during the initial stages of life. The term 'learning' was used throughout the inquiry to refer to 'all forms of organised education and training (whether or not they carry certification)' (2009: 9–10). So, in this instance, formal or informal learning is learning that is facilitated and, in the case of formal learning, certificated.

Exploring lifelong learning, the inquiry recognised the range and diversity of meanings and interpretations that are given to the term across the literature, recognising the confusion surrounding its meaning. The confusion seems to arise from wanting to place lifelong learning in a 'box', with tidy purposes and ages attributable to it (Schuller and Watson, 2009).

In combined formal and informal types of learning they developed a broad definition for lifelong learning:

> Lifelong learning includes people of all ages learning in a variety of contexts – in educational institutions, at work, at home and through leisure activities. It focuses mainly on adults returning to organised learning rather than on the initial period of education or on incidental learning.
>
> (Schuller and Watson, 2009: 10)

This definition provides some useful boundaries and distinctions for us as we start to think about a 'frame' for lifelong learning, enabling us to filter out some areas and develop a focus for discussion.

Jarvis is an influential thinker and writer in the field of lifelong learning, and when discussing it he suggests that the term is now a 'common, taken-for-granted concept in the educational and business worlds'. However, such an approach to the term has resulted in a range of understandings – and misunderstandings – resulting in lifelong learning becoming 'a social ambiguity' (2011: 9). For Jarvis engagement in lifelong learning results in: some form of change to the participant; can be accounted for as a social change; and can be short term or permanent. This is a useful way of thinking about lifelong learning.

Definitions for lifelong learning then vary, but in essence they have some link with economic or social activity, and change. While lifelong learning is recognised as occurring over time, the concept has become synonymous with adult learning and has an element of skills development. The contradiction of using the terms 'learning' and 'skills' should not go unquestioned here. The terminology used in association with lifelong learning, as we have seen, has moved over time from one of education, to learning, to skills, and again acts to highlight the value of particular types of learning within our society at a given time in history.

Lifelong learning, it can be argued, is a straightforward concept – learning occurs as one goes through life (Cottle, 2011) – and there is a level of 'taken-for-grantedness' about lifelong learning; about what it is and what it means, as it is arguably 'what humans do best' (Schuller and Watson, 2009: 7). However, as we can see from the above discussions, trying to pin down what lifelong learning actually is, what it means and to whom, is rather messy and multifaceted, with a lot of different layers and different people involved. Lifelong learning appears to have associated with it opportunities for radicalisation and empowerment (Freire, 1996); economic success as well as benefits for health and well-being (Bynner et al., 2001); for personal interest; to provide opportunities for progression; to validate work experiences or sporting achievements; or as a coercive act where people are required to engage in learning for external purposes – for example, to receive welfare benefits or as part of work training programme.

Summary

This chapter has introduced you to some of the key concepts associated with lifelong learning, and has attempted to work towards a definition of lifelong learning that encompasses the needs and demands of contemporary UK society. Throughout this chapter, you have had the opportunity to consider some of the guiding concepts associated with lifelong learning, including *adult, learning, education, training* and *globalisation*.

The following chapter introduces you to the policy landscape that has informed and framed lifelong learning over the last two decades. It is important to recognise that lifelong learning is a very politically driven instrument, and the next chapter explores some of the key policy decisions over the last two decades that have informed, and formed, the framework of lifelong learning available in the UK today. However, it is important to recognise that lifelong learning is a fluid and ever-evolving concept – with different terminology being used to describe it and different areas gaining prominence – often associated with changing political focus, so the following chapter can only capture a moment in time. You should expect to review these policies in light of new and evolving policies going forward.

2

The development of lifelong learning in the UK
The policy context

Introduction

This chapter introduces you to the policy landscape that has informed the provision and delivery of lifelong learning in contemporary UK society. It aims to map out the key policies, starting from the arrival of the New Labour government in 1997, which governed the UK from 1997 to 2010, and follow this with the emerging lifelong learning policies being produced by the Coalition Liberal Democrat–Conservative government, elected in May 2010.

Once the policy landscape has been mapped, lifelong learning from a range of perspectives will be considered, asking:

- Who is involved in lifelong learning?
- What is being learnt in lifelong learning?
- Where is lifelong learning taking place?
- Who is facilitating lifelong learning: the lifelong learning workforce?

Lifelong learning: 1997 to 2010

When the Committee on Widening Participation, chaired by Baroness Helena Kennedy, presented their influential report *Learning Works* (Kennedy, 1997), it set out a radical vision to engage and draw back into learning those who, traditionally, had not taken advantage of educational opportunities. The focus was particularly on those with no, or inadequate, qualifications, suggesting that a return to learning offered opportunities to break free from cycles of economic disadvantage and social exclusion. Implicit in the report was the notion that individuals who find themselves considered as 'inadequately qualified', 'economically deprived' or 'socially excluded' agreed with such statements and wanted to 'break free' from such an existence. However, it is not clear in the report whether anybody actually asked them.

1997 saw the election of New Labour. One of the key campaign slogans used during the party's lobbying for election was 'education, education, education', with Tony Blair stating that 'Education is the best economic policy we have' (Labour Party, 1995). This campaign saw a significant step change in political thinking about education as a mechanism through which the UK could maintain, enhance and improve its economic prosperity and position within the global market. In presenting their account of a new learning age, the Department for Education and Employment stated that:

> Learning is the key to prosperity – for each of us as individuals, as well as for the nation as a whole. Investment in human capital will be the foundation of success in the knowledge-based global economy of the twenty-first century ... Learning through life will build human capital by encouraging the acquisition of knowledge and skills and emphasising creativity and imagination, the fostering of an enquiring mind and the love of learning are essential to our future.
>
> (DfEE, 1998)

The above quote is worth spending a little time unravelling. In this quote the Labour government clearly positions education – and learning – as a central focus for their political activity. They are outlining how learning opportunities will enable the UK to be economically successful as the economic market of the country changes from an industrial one, which relied heavily on manual labour and skills, to a service-led economy relying on technology and higher-level knowledge and skills.

In order to have a population who can engage effectively in such an economy, investment in learning and potentially a cultural shift – from thinking about learning as stopping with the end of compulsory schooling at 16 to perceiving it as an activity in which people continually engage – was required. The ambition for the government was to 'sell' learning as something everyone would want to engage in, with the consequence of having a population who were more highly skilled and able to participate in higher-level jobs – having the resultant effect of increasing the human capital available within the country. Human capital is a concept widely associated with economic activity and often associated with having people available who are economically active (for a further discussion around human capital see Chapter 4 on higher education).

Following the successful election of the New Labour government in 1997, the next decade saw the introduction of a swath of policies associated with education and lifelong learning. Below are a few of the key documents introduced that significantly influenced the direction of lifelong learning opportunities in the UK:

DfEE (1998) *The Learning Age: A Renaissance for a New Britain*, London: The Stationery Office.

This document set the scene for learning under a New Labour government that aimed to develop a culture of learning for the UK that would mark a step change in the provision of learning, moving lifelong learning to a central position in government thinking and investment.

DfEE (2001a) *Skills for Life: The National Strategy for Improving Adult Literacy and Numeracy Skills,* London: The Stationery Office.

This was a significant, flagship strategy of the New Labour government that saw the biggest investment in lifelong learning and a swath of activity. Essentially, this strategy aimed to ensure that all adults in the UK were given the opportunity to engage in learning programmes to develop their literacy and numeracy skills. This had the dual ambition of ensuring adults had the necessary skills to be able to participate in knowledge-based employment and also were more able to engage in society more generally.

DfES (2002a) *Success for All: Reforming Further Education and Training: Our Vision for the Future*, London: Stationery Office.

This document focused particularly on the relationships between further education and training, aiming to ensure closer working relationships between post-compulsory learning providers and employers to ensure that adults were learning the necessary skills to be able to gain employment in the areas where employers were struggling to recruit because of a lack of skills.

DfES (2003a) *21st Century Skills: Realising Our Potential*, London: Stationery Office.

This document provided an outline of the range of future skills required by employers to ensure a prosperous economy for the next decade and, as such, the focus and priority of the learning programmes that should be made available.

DfES (2005) *Skills: Getting On in Business, Getting On at Work*, Cm 6483-11, London: Stationery Office.

Again, we can see from this document the step-change in lifelong learning – arguably moving from a historical social 'good' with a focus on social justice and personal development to one with a focus on skills development and crucially, association with economic activity and human capital acquisition.

Foster, A. (2005) *Realising the Potential: A Review of the Future Role of Further Education Colleges*, DfES, London: The Stationery Office.

Foster's review of further education colleges, as a significant provider of lifelong learning opportunities, focused particularly on raising the standards of programmes being delivered, and the workforce delivering them, to ensure that provision was of a high enough quality to meet the continuing demands of employers.

DfES (2006) *Further Education: Raising Skills, Improving Life Chances*, London: The Stationery Office.

This document provides a brief respite from the demanding focus on skills acquisition for employment, recognising that by engaging in learning opportunities life chances could be enhanced. However, the overarching focus suggests that life chances necessarily require increased skills to be improved.

Leitch, S. (2006) *Leitch Review of Skills: Prosperity for All in the Global Economy – World Class Skills*, London: Stationery Office.

This was an influential report that outlined the limitations and preparedness of the country to be able to compete in a global market, and made significant recommendations for the development of the sector.

DIUS (2007) *World Class Skills: Implementing the Leitch Review of Skills in England*, London: Stationery Office.

This report outlined the government's response to the Leitch report and set out a revised set of ambitions of skills achievement for England. The report set out a series of strategic actions and interventions in order to implement the recommendations outlined in the Leitch Report.

The next decade saw the demise of the New Labour government, with the new political landscape being led by a new Liberal Democrat–Conservative Coalition government.

Lifelong learning: 2010 to mid-2012

We have already seen, during the period of the New Labour government, a change in the use of terminology from 'education' and 'learning' to one of 'skills'. In May 2010, the election of a Liberal Democrat–Conservative Coalition government saw a refocusing and reframing of the lifelong learning sector, perhaps most significantly through its renaming as the 'future education and skills' sector. This perhaps seemingly innocuous change of wording clearly locates the ambitions of the new government and signals their view on the purpose of lifelong learning, closely aligning it with engagement for the purpose of skills acquisition rather that what now might seem to be a distant vision for the sector posed by the DfEE (1998) a decade earlier, of 'a learning age' that appeared to embrace learning of all types and the ambition to develop a culture of learning. The sector, to date, has been significantly influenced by the direction of a series of policy and strategy documents, not least because the supporting funding frameworks generally follow the policy focus.

The seminal strategy published by the government in November 2010 was the *Skills for Sustainable Growth* strategy (DBIS, 2010b). In this document, the government recognises that:

> Skills are vital to our future and improving skills is essential to building sustainable growth and stronger communities. A skilled workforce is necessary to stimulate the private-sector growth that will bring new jobs and new prosperity for people all over this country.
>
> And a strong further education and skills system is fundamental to social mobility, re-opening routes for people from where they begin to succeed in work, become confident through becoming accomplished and play a full part in civil society.
>
> (DBIS, 2010b: 3)

What is evident from the above introductory quote to this strategy document – jointly provided by Vince Cable, Secretary of State for Business, Innovation and Skills and

John Hayes, Minister of State for Further Education, Skills and Lifelong Learning – is that the system of lifelong learning, under the governance of the Coalition, appears to be driven by a skill acquisition agenda that has the ambition of ensuring that a skilled workforce is available to contribute to the economic buoyancy of the country. There is also recognition that such skill acquisition could enable social mobility – a term used to refer to the capacity of an individual to move through ingrained societal class structures.

The strategy was built using three guiding principles of fairness, responsibility and freedom:

Fairness
We believe those first in line for help must be those least able to help themselves. So we are paying special attention to young people and those without basic literacy and numeracy skills.

Responsibility
Whilst government has a role employers and citizens must take greater responsibility for ensuring their own skills needs are met.

Freedom
Freedom does not just mean abolishing stifling bureaucracy and meaningless targets. It means trusting people to do their job. The adult education movement was not born of Government, but of the people. And its primary accountability today should not be to Government, but to the people it serves.

(DBIS, 2010b: 3)

This seminal document has framed the evolving landscape of lifelong learning for the contemporary UK and we will explore the influence of this strategy on each strand of the sector throughout this book. However, it is worth noting that these guiding principles move responsibility and accountability for engaging in learning away from government and lay them directly at the feet of the individual – which is arguably a good thing. However, the associated funding strategy, published alongside this document (DBIS, 2010a) does raise some interesting questions around the potential for people to invest in their own training, and the resultant influence on an individual's debt that engagement in learning is likely to create.

It is important, however, to acknowledge that while government is principally focused on supporting learning that leads to economic prosperity, that is not to say it does not continue to recognise the importance of other lifelong learning opportunities. This is evidenced, for example, through the continued support of adult and community learning projects.

Reflection

Having read the outline of the policies under the different political parties, see if you can identify any key differences between the parties' perspectives on their ambitions for lifelong learning provision.

Summary

Lifelong learning appears, over recent decades, to have become a central element of government action, as they have recognised lifelong learning as a tool to improve the position of the UK both economically and socially within a global market.

Successive policy documents presented by the New Labour government, throughout their governance, focus heavily on the need to build a learning society (Hodgson and Spours, 1999), with all individuals having an entitlement to lifelong learning. It can be argued that the centralisation and focus of lifelong learning as a potential tool for social justice during the New Labour government resulted from a recognition by them that changing labour markets were creating the further marginalisation and exclusion of individuals who lacked the basic skills needed to engage in society – particularly literacy and numeracy (Hodgson and Spours, 1999). The development of a shared responsibility to engage in lifelong learning, and the shared benefits of engaging in lifelong learning, are key components of such an approach, with the state, employers and individuals all playing a significant role in this approach, implying both expectations and obligations for all parties concerned. This three-point responsibility approach has been adopted by the Liberal Democrat–Conservative Coalition, as seen above, and developed with a new framework for funding lifelong learning.

Government policies increasingly identify lifelong learning as the foundation upon which individuals can advance their employability and contribute to the creation of a competitive economic market. This human capital view of lifelong learning has led to vast levels of government investment in education and training (knowledge and skills), although some might argue (Schuller and Watson, 2009) that this is actually a 'drop in the ocean'. For example, during the first half of the last decade, the then New Labour government spend some £1.6 billion on the implementation of the *Skills for Life* strategy (DfEE, 2001a). That said, governments, both New Labour and the subsequent Coalition, also identify education and training as important concepts in the creation of social justice[1] (HM Government, 2012).

Funding of and for lifelong learning is an important area for discussion when thinking about lifelong learning – particularly who should pay, when and why. As we go through each chapter of this book, and consider the various strands of lifelong learning, we will explore how funding influences the lifelong learning chances and opportunities of individuals in the UK.

Who is involved in lifelong learning?

The simple answer to this question is everyone! However, as I hope is now apparent, nothing is that easy in lifelong learning. You are engaged in lifelong learning if you are undertaking training as part of your work commitments; if you have decided to join a horse-riding club; if you are engaged in graduate or postgraduate study; if you are involved in a training programme to aid recovery from a health diagnosis, such as mental ill health or bereavement; or if you are unemployed and attending a welfare training programme. The ambitions of government to create a society that is built on a 'culture of learning' could be said to be evident – and learning of all kinds appears to be available at all levels and in many locations.

That said, people engaging in lifelong learning are often 'grouped' or labelled as, for example: learners with learning difficulties and disability (LLDD); learners who are not in education, employment and training (NEET); older-aged; socially excluded; members of gangs; those with a mental ill-health diagnosis; people of religion and belief; English speakers of other languages (ESOL); family learners; and the unemployed. This is by no means an exhaustive list. What I hope is apparent, though, is the identification of people who could be considered to be 'socially excluded' or vulnerable members of society who are unable to navigate mainstream society successfully. As we go through each chapter of this book, we will consider how such groups engage and participate in lifelong learning, and the role of lifelong learning as an opportunity for social justice.

What is being learnt in lifelong learning?

The types of curriculum being delivered through lifelong learning can be divided into learning that is provided for public good and learning that is provided for personal good. Lifelong learning for public good, and supported by the national purse, arguably provides a curriculum that has an economic ambition, with lifelong learning for personal good being funded by the individual with a broader curriculum beyond economic potential. However, such polarisation of purpose should be challenged as it has the potential to create a hierarchy of access to learning, which is fuelled by the ability to pay to engage in learning. Again, this will be a topic of debate as we consider each sector of lifelong learning in subsequent chapters.

Where is lifelong learning taking place?

Lifelong learning can be considered to be an umbrella term to describe learning that occurs in our society. However, similarly to compulsory schooling being identified as early years, primary and secondary stages of learning, through which young people traverse chronologically by age, the lifelong learning sector can be considered to be divided into strands of learning. These are not identified by ages but by purpose and focus and include: adult and community learning; further education; higher education; work-based learning; and prison and probation strands.

Each of these strands of the sector form the basis for discussion of lifelong learning throughout this book. However, it is important to recognise that these strands have been constructed for ease of discussion and often the boundaries of lifelong learning are apparent across strands. For example, prisoners engage in higher education and many further education programmes are offered through the workplace, or in community settings.

Who is facilitating lifelong learning: the lifelong learning workforce?

The lifelong learning teaching workforce, who facilitate lifelong learning, are an important area of focus for the sector, as they not only facilitate the provision of lifelong learning but also form part of the sector itself.

Those of you who are reading this book, or intending to read parts of it, are likely to have come into contact with a member of the lifelong learning workforce, whether through formal learning undertaken at college, or as a facilitator of learning in a workplace. Perhaps you have undertaken some volunteering and have been trained to deliver your volunteering, or perhaps you have supported learning in some less formal way, for example at your local church or swimming club, or the local Scouts group. Whatever area you have engaged in, or encountered some learning, that facilitator of learning is a member of the lifelong learning workforce.

The lifelong learning teaching workforce is, like the sector, diverse. Historically, the sector has drawn its workforce from industry. For many people working in the sector, this is a second career, often following on from their initial profession (Cara, et al., 2010) whether that is business, such as accounting or management, or vocational, such as hairdressing, catering or construction, for example. These individuals are identified as having expertise in their first profession as well as holding a position where they are able to 'pass on' the knowledge of their profession. Perhaps surprisingly, unlike teachers working in the 'compulsory' sector, the teaching workforce of the lifelong learning sector have (until recently) not been compulsorily required to hold a teaching qualification of any kind – as a result, the quality of teaching was often varied and fragmented (Ofsted, 2003).

At the beginning of the millennium, the Institute for Employment Studies (Maginn and William, 2002) undertook an assessment of the skills needs of teachers working in the lifelong learning sector. Their findings identified a need for an increase in basic skills teaching and training, as well as mechanisms for the transferability of qualifications across the sector. Following the renewed interest and investment in post-16 education by the New Labour government in 1997, there was a targeted focus on the professionalisation of the lifelong learning teaching workforce at part of a wider strategy aimed at reforming the sector. This government made it a mandatory requirement that all those responsible for teaching in the sector should hold a teaching qualification. This move was further substantiated by a critical review of teaching standards across the sector by the Office for Standards in Education, Children's Services and Skills (Ofsted) in 2003.

As a result of a public consultation between November 2003 and February 2004, the then Department for Education and Skills (DfES, 2004) published *Equipping Our Teachers for the Future*, in which the government set out their plans for reforming initial teacher training within the sector. The aim of these reforms was to equip teachers with all the skills needed to teach for the future. The report outlined a step change in teacher education for the sector, introducing new minimum standards, a unit- and credit-based teacher qualifications framework, and additional professional status (QTLS). It was expected that these reforms would be operative by September 2007.

Initially, the government focused on members of the sector responsible for the delivery of literacy (English) and numeracy (mathematics), requiring that they hold both a teaching qualification and a specialist certificate of competence to deliver their chosen curriculum subject. This development was part of the government's *Skills for Life* strategy (DfEE, 2001a).

So, since the start of the millennium there has been a range of government initiatives and tools created, to support and frame the evolution of an effective professional teaching workforce for the lifelong learning sector.

Professionalism as a term is often used to identify a person who has expert knowledge, skills and understanding of a particular area of work. For the education sector, knowledge of teaching is generally regarded as the mechanism that identifies the profession as holding subject expertise. People who facilitate learning in the lifelong learning sector are variously identified as: lecturers, teachers, trainers, facilitators, practitioners, tutors, trainers or assessors. To avoid confusion, I will refer to this group as teachers.

The New Labour government charged Lifelong Learning UK (LLUK) – one of 22 sector skills councils established by the government – to take responsibility for the development and implementation of a series of professional standards for teachers in the lifelong learning sector, which should be achieved through the acquisition of a set of associated named qualifications.

At the start of the millennium, the size of the workforce was estimated to be between 800,000 and 1,200,000 (LLUK, 2007). Additionally, there were significant numbers of volunteers working particularly in the adult and community learning strand of the sector. The aim of the new standards was to ensure that:

> individuals working within the LLUK footprint have access to qualifications which not only encourage development and progression, but also recognise and reflect the skills and knowledge achieved at all stages in an individual's career.
>
> (LLUK, 2007: 3)

In developing the framework, four ambitious outcomes were identified by LLUK on behalf of the government: (1) improving education and training participation and attainment among young people aged 14–19; (2) improving literacy and numeracy and increasing qualifications levels in the working-age population; (3) increasing social inclusion and improving individuals' employability; and (4) lifelong learning system reform and quality improvement.

From 1 September 2007, new teachers entering the lifelong learning sector were required to hold or acquire one of the following qualifications within a specified period of time:

- A 'Preparing to Teach in the Lifelong Learning Sector' (PTLLS) award (or its equivalent), which was a minimum threshold licence to teach for anyone who had an element of teaching in their role, irrespective of job title; and

- A Diploma in Teaching in the Lifelong Learning Sector at minimum Level 5 (or its equivalent) leading to Qualified Teacher Learning and Skills (QTLS) status for those in a full teaching role; or

- A Certificate in Teaching in the Lifelong Learning Sector at Level 3 or 4 (or its equivalent), leading to Associate Teacher Learning and Skills (ATLS) status for those in an associate teaching role, (i.e. a role that carries significantly less than the full range of teaching responsibilities carried out in a full teaching role); and

- To complete a period of professional formation, (the post-qualification process by which a teacher demonstrates, through professional practice, that they meet the professional standards and can effectively apply the skills and knowledge acquired during teacher training).

Prior to these reforms, those working as a teacher in the lifelong learning sector could elect to work towards a varied and mixed range of qualifications. These new programmes aimed to provide a clear programme of qualification requirements for the varying teaching roles identified throughout the sector.

Once teachers had achieved their initial teaching qualifications, they were then expected to work towards professional formation, or QTLS, in order to achieve a license to practice. This process was overseen through the Institute of Learning – a new membership organisation for the sector.

For *Skills for Life* teachers, with responsibility for teaching literacy, numeracy and language, since the publication of the *Moser Report* (DfEE, 1999) and the *Skills for Life* strategy (DfEE, 2001a) there has been a sustained focus on the professional development of this strand of the workforce. This saw the implementation of, initially Level 4 subject specialist certificates for *Skills for Life* teachers in each of the specialist areas, and subsequently, alongside the 2007 reforms, the introduction of Level 5 diplomas for each of the *Skills for Life* specialist areas.

These changes were largely welcomed and embraced by the sector workforce. However, a range of challenges and issues – both for the providers of initial teacher training qualifications and by institutions and individuals trying to navigate the system to ensure they access the most appropriate programme – have been experienced (O'Grady, 2009).

The implementation of a robust framework, it was expected, would result in a comprehensive suite of courses being offered by providers to meet the new requirements. However, there is evidence from some initial research by Ofsted (2010) that both the supply of qualified teachers to the workforce, and the access to professional courses, appears somewhat disjointed and fractured.

The development of 14–19 Diplomas (these will be discussed in Chapter 5 on further education), which overlap traditional teaching boundaries (compulsory up to the age of 16, and post-compulsory teaching), have 'greyed' the boundaries for which these qualifications were built. The new LLUK-approved qualification enables a qualified teacher to work in traditional post-compulsory settings; however, many new models of lifelong learning teaching and learning take place in the compulsory setting.

The replacement of the Learning and Skills Council, which funded all post-16 education and training, with a range of new funding agencies (the Skills Funding Agency, the National Apprenticeship Service and the Young People's Learning Agency) in April 2010, to fund learning programmes across different age strands, added further layers of complexity to understanding the purpose and place of the newly developed lifelong learning teaching qualifications.

Evidence from a recent study (O'Grady, 2009) suggests there is a range of challenges and issues emerging – both for the providers of teacher training programmes and for those who are wishing to access teacher training programmes as a result of the 2007 reforms – that need to be addressed.

Throughout the development of the teacher qualification initiatives there is an acknowledgment that in order to ensure the success of the sector in achieving the ambitions set out for it through successive government policies, it is imperative to ensure that the workforce is supported so that it can grow in both capacity and capability. Additionally, there is recognition that the lifelong learning sector plays a critical role in supporting and enabling both social justice goals and outcomes, alongside economic prosperity, for both individuals and the country in positioning themselves within a global market.

At the time of writing (summer 2012), the sector waits, with some level of concern and anticipation, for the outcome of a six-month-long consultation and review of the lifelong learning workforce, chaired by Lord Lingfield – the Independent Review of Professionalism – which is due to report at the end of July 2012. The committee have put forward a series of recommendations in thinking about the reformation of the workforce, which include a 'rolling back' of the requirement of the lifelong learning teaching workforce to hold a professional teaching qualification, preferring instead to empower members of the workforce to decided whether, and at what level, they wish to obtain qualifications. Additionally, the committee suggests the removal of the statutory obligation for all members of the lifelong learning teaching workforce to register with the Institute for Learning (IfL) as part of their professional formation. Instead, they suggest that potential entrants to the profession should be offered discretionary advice regarding the range of qualifications and continuing professional development opportunities available to them. The findings of this committee are likely to have long-standing implications and ramifications for the workforce of the sector.

Reflection

What are your views about teachers of lifelong learning? Do you think all teachers facilitating lifelong learning should be expected to hold some teacher training qualifications? For all types of learning? What about facilitators of sports activities, such as yoga or swimming? Should qualifications only be held when qualifications are attached to the learning programme?

In thinking about the type of lifelong learning we currently have in the UK, it is apparent that there is an attempt to provide a framework for lifelong learning that offers opportunities for all members of society to be involved at any level.[2] However, it is also evident that the premise on which this is currently established by the Coalition – in terms of freedom, fairness and responsibility – has the potential to limit people's access to and engagement in lifelong learning.

An inclusive vision of lifelong learning proposed by Atkin (2000) argues that, as learning involves the extension of human potential it should be seen as 'an intrinsically worthwhile endeavour' (Atkin, 2000: 5), and one worthy of investment in its own right without any direct association with economic values.

Such an approach to lifelong learning might support a humanistic perspective of lifelong learning – that humans are naturally inquisitive and, as such, will be drawn to engage in learning opportunities. However, Kerka argues that adult learning as a voluntary activity is mythical and asserts that 'learning society rhetoric, financial incentives, and employer and social pressures are resulting in a new form of compulsory learning, learning as a "life sentence": a new form of social control' (2000: 5). These views of emergent coercive frameworks of engagement in lifelong learning are supported in the work of Coffield (1999) and Illeris (2003a). Illeris concluded, from his research exploring the engagement in learning by adults, that:

> the main result of our investigating adult education from the perspective of ordinary learners who are alien to such concepts as lifelong learning and lifelong education

is that if it is given to or forced upon participants who have not mentally accepted and internalized a wish or need to acquire the knowledge, skills, attitudes or qualities in question, it will tend to be a waste of human and financial resources.

(Illeris, 2003a: 22)

These different perspectives offer challenges for us as we think about why and how people participate in lifelong learning.

3

Adult and community learning

Introduction

This chapter will focus on lifelong learning from the perspective of adult and community learning. Having read the previous chapter, you are now familiar with the challenges of thinking about what an adult is, and what it means to be called an adult. In this chapter we consider the concept of 'community' – what does this mean and, in particular, what does this mean when we are talking about community lifelong learning?

Broadly, we are focusing on groups of people who share a particular interest or hobby, or specific groups that could be considered to be 'socially constructed' by our society – the poor, the unemployed, the uneducated, gang members, NEETs (not in employment, education or training) and migrants, to name just a few. The concept of community is widely used in the literature to explain a variety of communities. This chapter will explore the concept of community, particularly from a lifelong learning perspective, and consider how it has been influenced by policy and politicians, and how it has changed over time.

For this chapter, we are going to focus on lifelong learning for social benefits, and for wider benefits, beyond a focus on economic outcomes, and explore where such learning opportunities occur in the community and whether they have at their heart a particular community agenda.

Over the last two decades, there has been an increasing focus on social learning – that is, learning that has the ambition to support social justice, and create active and engaged societies who have adopted and developed a culture of learning – through community learning. This can be seen in government discussions on the value and benefits of engaging in social learning and its transformative opportunities through, for example, the creation of the Transformative Fund (DIUS, 2009) to support informal adult learning by the New Labour government. More recently, the Coalition government has continued this through the adoption of the 'Big Society' agenda (Office for Civil Society, 2010), with an enhanced focus of the role of the 'third sector' in providing and supporting learning opportunities to develop a sense of civic responsibility within communities, and most recently through the funding of Community Learning Trusts (DBIS, 2012) that aim to inspire people to engage in learning. In launching the scheme, John Hayes, currently the Skills Minister, reaffirmed the Coalition government's commitment to supporting learning of all types when he commented that 'Learning is the lifeblood of personal and economic growth in our local communities' (DBIS, 2012), and acknowledged that by engaging in learning there are opportunities to transform people's attitudes and abilities, and bring communities together to nurture a common good.

The questions for consideration in this chapter then include: what is the role and contribution of 'community' in lifelong learning? Who participates in adult and community learning? And who are the stakeholders that provide and support adult and community lifelong learning opportunities?

A word about terminology

As is a common challenge with all areas of lifelong learning, the terms used to describe adult and community learning have gone through various iterations, so in the literature you may find it referred to as *adult safeguarded learning*, *informal adult learning*, *third sector learning*, and *voluntary community learning*. While there are likely to be some semantic differences between each of these terms, the commonalities, for me, significantly outweigh the differences. For the purposes of this discussion, I will refer to the strand as adult and community learning.

What is a community?

You might start reading this section by thinking this is an obvious question with an obvious answer – but if I said that a community might refer to a group of people who are sharing the experience of mental ill-health, or sharing a prison wing, or sharing space in a residential home, would that challenge your thinking?

'Community' has a range of associations when used in conjunction with lifelong learning. Lifelong learning, or adult education, was born within a social justice movement by socially and politically motivated activists who met to share a common discussion or debate. The establishment of such learning activity is the embodiment of adult learning, leading to the creation of the Workers' Education Association (WEA). Members of a community are considered as such because they share common identifiers, whether they are gang members who all share their membership through symbols such as tattoos, or groups who share a common experience: for example, those who are NEET, or perhaps are being typed as a teenage mother, as substance dependent, as sharing a mental ill-health diagnosis, or being identified by an age indicator (such as older learners who come together to engage in learning through the University of the Third Age – a voluntary organisation to enable people over the age of 55 to engage in joint learning or discussion groups).

What is clear is that 'community' is a social construct with varying competing definitions that can be located by place – geographical, spatial, cultural, ethical, network, market; by close association – of values, solidarity, commitment, mutuality and trust, fraternity, fellowship; or by a set of interests with a set of common characteristics or variables – such as sexual orientation, occupation, religious belief or ethnic origin.

The unifying link for the notion of 'community' is that there is a shared common identity. The most well-known global communities to emerge in recent society, for example, are cyber-based and include Facebook and Twitter in which people with particular shared interests can communicate.

Lave and Wenger (1991) developed the concept of community to an active agent, conceptualised as a 'community of practice'. Wenger (1998) describes a community of practice as an 'organic space' (something that can grow, change and evolve over time) where learning can happen and is based on four fundamental premises: that we are all social beings, which is considered to be a central aspect of learning; that knowledge is a matter of competence and should be linked to the value of the experience; that knowing is a matter of participating and so requires active engagement in the world; and that meaning is derived from the ability to experience the world and so make our engagement meaningful.

Wenger, in presenting his construct of 'community', develops a theory of learning that starts with an assumption: engagement in social practice is the fundamental process by which we learn and so become who we are. This main element of exploration neither focuses on individual or social institutions, but rather on informal 'communities of practice' that people form as they pursue shared enterprises over time. Such an approach allows you to think about learning as a process of social participation and absolutely informs the models of learning provision within the adult and community learning strand of the lifelong learning sector.

What is community learning?

So, now we understand a little more about the notion of community, we need to consider what, then, is community learning? Community learning emerged as a model of learning from a range of influential twentieth-century social thinkers on education, such as Dewey (1916) and Knowles (1975) who are considered to be the 'godfathers' of adult education and who framed the form through which effective models of adult education were delivered (see Chapter 1 for a discussion on the notion of adult, and adult education). For those engaged in this type of learning, either as a participant or provider, the learning often has a social justice element – for example, a 'second chance' to gain qualifications or to undertake learning that, for whatever reason, was missed during the compulsory stage of education.

The model of delivering adult education was developed by Knowles (1975), and followed on from the work of Houle (1964) and Tough (1967). Named the andragogical approach to learning, and advocated by Knowles et al. (2005), this model suggested that the teacher prepare in advance a set of procedures for involving learners in a process involving the following elements (Knowles et al., 2005: 115):

1. Preparing the learner;
2. Establishing a climate conducive to learning;
3. Creating a mechanism for mutual planning;
4. Diagnosing the needs for learning;
5. Formulating programme objectives (which is content) that will satisfy these needs;
6. Designing a pattern of learning experiences;

7. Conducting these learning experiences with suitable techniques and materials; and

8. Evaluating the learning outcomes and re-diagnosing learning needs.

The distinction made between this approach to facilitating learning for adults is that is it is based on a *process model*, rather than a more traditional approach to teaching for younger people which is arguably considered to be a *content* model.

Adult and community learning: social exclusion/inclusion and social justice

The concept of social justice can be located at the heart of lifelong learning, and is most acutely evidenced in this strand of lifelong learning. Social justice can be considered as an umbrella term and, like many other terms, it reflects an ecological development in our use of language.

During the New Labour government, terms such as 'social exclusion' were used to explain, understand and develop policies, interventions and strategy responses for members of society who were identified or considered to be 'excluded' from mainstream activity. Over the life of their government, thinking moved from an exclusionary model to an inclusive model, and the term 'social inclusion' became the preferred terminology in literature when thinking about marginalisation or disadvantage.

In developing an overarching definition for social exclusion, the United Nations identified that social exclusion could be said to exist at a national level when there was evidence of a lack of income and productive resources to enable sustainable livelihoods, incorporating: hunger and malnutrition; ill health; homelessness; social discrimination; and, importantly for our discussion, limited or lack of access to education (Rodgers et al., 1995). Social exclusion can be further characterised by lack of participation in decision making and in civil, social and cultural life (United Nations, 1995).

The election of the New Labour government in 1997 saw a centralised cross-government focus on social exclusion in our society, evidenced by the creation of the Social Exclusion Unit. In developing a definition for social exclusion they positioned social exclusion as:

> a shorthand label for what can happen when individuals or areas suffer from a combination of linked problems such as unemployment, poor skills, low incomes, poor housing, high crime environments, bad health and family breakdown.
>
> (SEU, 1997)

The objective for the Social Exclusion Unit was to create prosperous, inclusive and sustainable communities for the twenty-first century; places where people wanted to live and that promoted both opportunity and a better quality of life for all. The Unit was actively engaged in programmes and projects until its replacement in 2006 with a smaller Social Exclusion Taskforce. The election of the Coalition government in 2010 saw the closure of this Taskforce, with their work being transferred to the Office for Civil Society and being subsumed in the work of the Big Society (Office for Civil Society, 2010).

The term 'social inclusion' can be said to be the antithesis of 'social exclusion' and can arguably be identified as a more positive model and response to poverty and disadvantage, as opposed to the deficit approach adopted by social exclusion. Inclusion, according to Sen (2000) is characterised by a society's widely shared social experience and active participation, by a broad equality of opportunities and life chances for individuals and by the achievement of a basic level of well-being for all citizens.

The term 'social justice' is currently the most contemporary phrase used in the literature, adopted by the Coalition when thinking about how to tackle and eradicate disadvantage, born particularly out of poverty. In their recently published document *Social Justice: Transforming Lives* (HM Government, 2012), the government asserts that 'Social justice is about making society function better – providing the support and tools to help turn lives around' (2012: 1). This term sits alongside a parallel government priority of increasing the 'social mobility' of the population. The *Strategy for Social Mobility* (Cabinet Office, 2011) aims to empower people to move 'up the social ladder', with the above social justice strategy being the precursor strategy that aims to give people the capacity in terms of skills to put their 'foot on that ladder'.

In developing these strategies, there is recognition by government that education plays a significant role in creating a more just society, with evidence that low educational attainment is closely associated with lower incomes, unemployment, poorer health and increased criminality. The role of lifelong learning, then, can be seen to contribute to these government agendas.

There is much to explore in the literature regarding these concepts, and you are strongly advised to read, for example, the work of Ruth Levitas (2005) and Hilary Silver (1994) who provide some very interesting theoretical models for thinking about social exclusion, in order to develop a critical understanding of these concepts and their relationship to the provision of lifelong learning programmes and intervention. What is evident is that educational attainment is an effective predictor of adult life outcomes, with poor levels of educational attainment and basic skills as children creating a higher risk of social exclusion as adults.

The role of lifelong learning as an enabler to facilitate socially constructed groups to become participants in mainstream society is the focus of lifelong learning provision for all strands of the sector, but perhaps more so for this strand.

Learning in adult and community learning

When we start to think about what learning is, how we learn and how we can measure learning, it is then worth reflecting on the fact that learning is a process which we are engaged in all the time. Sometimes it is formalised, which is often identified in our society through formal assessments or tests which are measured and certificated. Often, though, learning is less apparent, but just as important and significant. Frequently community learning is associated with this type of learning – called learning for self, or informal learning.

There is a diverse range of learning theorists who have both developed and explored learning from a range of perspectives, putting emphasis on different elements involved in the process of learning, whether that is cognition, emotion or society (Illeris, 2004). Illeris argues that while the concept of learning covers all processes that lead to a relatively lasting change of capacity, in fact learning exists within a tension field which varies depending on the purpose and focus of learning. Learning, he asserts, should be seen as a concept which integrates and draws on a range of elements incorporating inclusive practice learning, collective learning and development learning to build a learning organisation.

While lifelong learning within a community framework aims to enable each individual to be involved in the learning process, their focus generally starts with individuals as part of a community – building a network of support to enable individuals to persist, progress and achieve with their learning endeavour. This approach supports Wenger's (1998) social theory of learning – that is, that learning should largely be organised on the assumption that learning is an individual process, but that engagement is for the most part a socially interactive experience.

Adult and community learning: diversity

Within neighbourhoods, people differ in many ways. The nature of diversity in British communities is noted by McNair (2008) to have changed in two particular ways – through increasing polarisation, particularly seen for example in terms of age mix, wealth, social engagement and political activity; and the rise of 'super-diversity', with neighbourhoods increasingly including people from a wide range of different backgrounds.

Learning in the community then, can take many forms and needs to be effective for a wide range of audiences, but is often built on a model that aims to enable the individual engaging in the learning experience to have a degree of power in controlling the type and direction of their learning, leading to ambitions of emancipation.

This makes curriculum management challenging. However, a challenge is something that the adult and community sector are familiar with. This is perhaps the most diverse strand of the lifelong learning sector but they are regarded as the strand that are most effective at working with, and supporting, people who find themselves isolated or excluded from mainstream society.

As we have seen above, learning has been identified as a major tool for reintegrating people back into mainstream society. The next section will introduce you to some groups in society who can be said to fall into the umbrella category of 'hard to reach', and with whom adult and community learning providers work effectively to support their reintegration into mainstream society through learning programmes. However, as a caveat, you should be aware that is only a small representation of the work of this strand of the sector.

Who are the providers and participants accessing adult and community learning?

Family learning programmes

There is significant evidence in the literature that 'family disadvantage can lay the foundation for poor literacy skills, limited education opportunities and restricted adult life changes, often manifested in social exclusion (Bynner, 2009) and that family learning should be identified as a key site where change can take place within neighbourhoods (Pahl, 2009).

Family learning aims to develop learning programmes that engage families and empower them, which can, in turn, be transformational. NIACE (online) advocate a vision of a '*learning* family' that seeks to embed a culture of learning where engagement in learning activity is normalised and every member of the family is a lifelong learner, aiming to create community well-being, economic prosperity and social cohesion. Family learning aims to support parents, grandparents, carers and other family members to be an active part of their children's learning experience, as well as becoming learners themselves. Learning can include many different types of activity, which can either develop specific academic knowledge (such as literacy or numeracy, leading to accredited qualifications), or to developing an understanding of helping children engage in play, reading, or working together as a family to develop, for example, a family history which does lead towards qualification outcomes. Generally, the learning is situated within the community and can take place in a range of locations, such as schools, children's centres, museums and libraries.

Effective family learning programmes, according to Pahl (2009), need to be meaningful and take place in a context that is both informed and takes into consideration the practices and routines of family life. These aspects are particularly important for those providing family learning programmes as they will need to consider, for example, the time that a programme is delivered: does it allow parents to drop children at school or nursery? Does it finish in time to allow children to be picked up? Can it be timetabled for a weekend to enable all family members to participate in the learning activity? Are there activities to engage all family members? Does the learning programme meet the potential needs of a family? For example, discussing family financing would need to include some numeracy activities for children across a range of ages and capabilities, and discussions would need to cover household budgeting and managing debt, again across a range of capabilities.

The success of family learning programmes, particularly in supporting children's education, in achieving positive outcomes both socially and economically is evidenced by sustained government support for such programmes. By engaging in family learning, adults can also improve their own personal self-confidence to engage in learning and improve their own skills. NIACE launched a new inquiry into family learning in September 2012, which aims to report in 2013 on the role, purpose and understanding of family learning going forward.

Programmes for those who are not in education employment or training (NEET)

The term 'NEET' has been adopted by politicians, media and academics alike, and has become embedded into our general language to refer to a group of young people who find themselves outside some of the key mainstream societal institutions of employment and education. However, you should question the term before we think about the role of adult and community learning for such learners. Can it be used as a homogeneous term? What does 'young' refer to? If a young person is choosing not to work because they are travelling, or they decide to take on caring responsibilities in a family they are, arguably, NEET in the way that we have come to use and understand this term. The term is often used as a derogatory phrase and can be said to be 'reductionist', in that it describes people who are not involved in mainstream activities, leading to their marginalisation and exclusion from mainstream services and resources. So, NEET should be seen as a concept that needs to mirror the dynamics of a young person's life (Parsons and Bynner, 2002).

So, it is important to think about who might find themselves included in a NEET definition. Currently, those who can acquire this label include young people who are: long-term unemployed (six months or more); fleetingly unemployed, looking after children or relatives in the home; temporarily sick or long-term disabled; or taking a short break from work or education. A helpful definition has been developed by NIACE as:

> those in the 16–24 age group who are eligible for but not participating in education, employment and/or training.
>
> (Dixon et al., 2011: 3)

By mid-2011, the number of NEET people had reached one million (ONS, online) with 16 per cent of this age group, 186,000 people, being aged between 16 and 18. This number is particularly worrying as NEET rates had been steadily decreasing from the mid-1980s, as participation in education expanded and there was economic growth. The rise in NEETs is thought to have developed following the development of a recession in the UK from 2008 and is a real concern for society, as having a period of being NEET can have a long-lasting influence on an individual's capacity to engage in mainstream society, leading for example to something termed by Lee and Wright (2011) as wage scarring – that is, the likelihood of lower earnings long after employment is found.

It is apparent that all those who attract the label NEET can be said to be disadvantaged. There are multiple subgroups of NEETs with varying experiences, characteristics and needs who require varying and different types of interventions – and this is where lifelong learning provision through the adult and community learning strand is effective.

It is clear that working with NEET groups is likely to require the recognition of multiple challenges that will take time to overcome. Many of the NEET community are transient, which means in practice that they often drop in and out of services because of the potential chaos of their lives, often characterised by complex needs and cycles of disadvantage. However, it is important that the NEET community are not homogenised. While it is often a focus for thinking about marginalisation and exclusion, for some this is an elective position not born of these indicators.

Current government initiatives to support those who are labelled NEET include a focus on learning, with, amongst other things, an entitlement of full fee remission up to the age of 24 to achieve or retake first full Level 2 or 3 qualifications, increases in apprenticeship opportunities, the development of a national careers service (and, importantly, support interventions through adult and community learning providers to increase employability skills by offering specific employability programmes), and programmes that offer stepping stones to further learning opportunities.

Reducing the number of NEETs in this country requires the coordination of activities of all key stakeholders (Lee and Wright, 2011). Additionally, financial support should be provided to locally embedded organisations, acknowledged as the 'third sector', that are best placed to positively engage with young people and the complexity of issues they face.

Programmes for gang members and individuals engaged in substance misuse and abuse

Increasingly, the Third Sector has been identified as those who are well placed to support people who find themselves, for whatever reason, marginalised from mainstream society, working with them to enable their reintegration into mainstream society and to improve their access to mainstream services. Linking lifelong learning to programmes that support a broader set of services with the potential to result in more diverse community engagement aligns with the ambitions of the Big Society (Office for Civil Society, 2010).

The rise in focus and concern by society of increased gang-related activity and substance dependence has resulted in a range of government-led initiatives and strategies to respond to these challenges. Adult and community learning providers play a crucial role in achieving successful outcomes for these initiatives.

The Coalition government launched their drug strategy (Home Office, 2010) with two key aims identified: to reduce the use of illicit and other harmful drugs, and to increase the numbers recovering from their dependence. In launching the strategy the government outlined a series of interventions, including programmes to prevent alcohol misuse through early intervention measures and paying attention to drugs and alcohol education.

Interestingly, drug use among 16–59 year olds is at its lowest level since measurement began in 1996. However, by the age of 15, 81 per cent of young people have had their first alcoholic drink, with 13,000 hospital admissions being recorded linked to young people's drinking and 15,000 accessing specialist support for alcohol misuse. The number of under-18s receiving help for alcohol use in 2010 was 8,227, while the number of under-18s in specialist substance misuse services in England was recorded as 23,582 (NTA, 2009/10). The drugs strategy (Home Office, 2010) identifies education as one of the most effective ways of preventing both drug and alcohol misuse, outlining the need for young people to have access to universal drug and alcohol education, linking closely with voluntary organisations, and playing a significant role in raising the awareness of the implications of substance misuse and abuse.

Gang members have often found themselves on the margins of society as a result of multiple challenges – both socially and economically. Such disadvantage can lead to limited engagement in compulsory schooling and a 'drifting' into gang communities and activity. Gang members often refer to their membership as a community who have shared common interests, values and beliefs. A range of explanations for the existence of gangs include the absence of positive role-models; poor parenting skills; a lack of diversionary activities; deprivation; family breakdown; absence of a father figure; a lack of morals and values; a lack of positive activities for young people living in neighbourhoods associated with gangs; and lack of aspiration. This can result in gang membership being seen as an attractive lifestyle, particularly because of the potential financial rewards. It is noteworthy that these explanations provide a deficit model of problems and challenges that leads to the blame for gang activity being laid firmly at the door of the family. It is for us to question whether alternative models for the explanation of gang membership and activity might exist – for example, the role of societal structures, including the institution of education.

Adult and community learning providers are well placed to provide a series of programmes to work with gang members who want to withdraw from their gang membership and reintegrate into mainstream society.

The profile of gang activity has also seen a recently raised profile as a result of a series of events, included increased incidence of gang-related crimes and teenage deaths, and the riot activity that covered the UK during August 2011. Reporting in 2009, the NASUWT (National Association of Schoolmasters and Union of Women Teachers) provided evidence that gang membership was closely associated with a culture of increasingly dangerous activity and violence, and that worryingly the average age of members was becoming younger.

In exploring the role of education in de-glamourising gang membership, and supporting people in getting out of such membership, NIACE in 2011 undertook some research into the reasons why people became members of gangs (Dixon et al., 2011) and found, perhaps unsurprisingly, a range of reasons for how people became involved in gang activity, including: poor experiences of school; feelings of alienation; low self-confidence; limited or no qualifications; lack of suitable job opportunities within their community; and personal problems or challenges and difficult home circumstances.

On 1 November 2011, the Coalition government launched an intensive prevention strategy to tackle the increasing challenge of gang membership entitled *Ending Gang and Youth Violence* (Home Office, 2011). This is a cross-government report that has developed a cross-government approach to tackling the challenge of gang and youth violence in the UK. The strategy identifies a range of vital stakeholders who will be instrumental in meeting the demands of the strategy, and teachers are identified as one of these stakeholders, alongside the police, doctors and youth workers.

The report, while acknowledging that the vast majority of young people are not involved in violence or gangs, also identified that membership increases the risk of serious violence and that gang membership results from entrenched educational and social failures.

The ambition of the strategy is to provide a series of 'pathways' out of violence and the gang culture, for young people wanting to make a break with this activity. Adopting a cross-government approach, key areas of focus have been established, and will be led by a newly created 'Ending Gang and Youth Violence Team'. Adult and community lifelong learning provision are well placed to support the roll-out of this strategy.

Health and well-being programmes

Adult and community learning programmes enable learners to engage in learning programmes to aid and enhance an individual's health and well-being. Examples of such programmes include those to assist learners with mental ill-health diagnoses.

Health, according to the World Health Organization's (WHO, 1948) can be defined as 'a state of complete physical, mental and social well-being and not merely the absence of disease or infirmity'. Evidence from the Foresight report (2008) concluded that there were diverse and long-term effects on individuals, families and society who experienced a mental ill-health diagnosis, and that they have a significant influence on the country's economic prosperity, as well as wider effects on well-being. NIACE (online) provide a wealth of evidence to demonstrate that one-in-four of the population will experience mental ill-health during their lifetime.

Health, happiness and well-being have become increasing areas of focus for government. As far back as 1973 a government committee identified that their work 'is of crucial importance for the health of our society and the quality of life of individual' citizens (DES, 1973: 20). Both the New Labour government and, subsequently, the Coalition government have invested resources in exploring the state of the nation's happiness. Indeed, the Coalition government inserted questions into the Census questionnaire completed nationally in March 2011 to measure well-being and happiness. The latest report, published in July 2012, highlights current happiness levels in England and continues to identify a relationship between engagement in employment and well-being.

There is a growing body of evidence to demonstrate that engaging in lifelong learning positively influences an individual's health and well-being. For example, McGivney (1999) found that participation in learning had a positive consequence for mental health, with Wheeler et al. (1999) highlighting two years later that some medical authorities were prescribing adult education courses as a treatment for some types of mental ill-health. Field (2008: 13), writing on the relationship between adult learning and well-being, argued that 'participation in adult learning appears to have some influence on attitudes and behaviors that affects people's mental well-being'. In his research he identified that on average people were more likely to experience greater well-being as a result of adult learning than not. While this relationship is relatively small, there is reasonable consistency in the literature to suggest that learning does impact positively upon a number of factors, such as employability and earnings, that in turn influence a person's well-being. Field (2008) concluded that engagement in lifelong learning provides tangible benefits, both directly and indirectly, for well-being.

Adult and community learning programmes for such learners are often built on a curriculum that focuses on the development of self-efficacy and self-confidence.

Adult and community learning programmes for migrant communities

The UK has seen a rise in migrant communities over the last two decades, partly in response to changes in cross-border arrangements. There are various ways in which a migrant can be identified: as an asylum seeker (someone who has arrived in the country to flee conflict or persecution from their country of original); as a failed asylum seeker (someone who's request for asylum has been rejected and who is awaiting repatriation to their country of origin); as a refugee (someone who has been granted leave to stay in the country); as an economic migrant (someone who has travelled legally from another country, generally EU countries, to seek work in the UK); or as an illegal immigrant (some who is staying in this country against the law) (Strategic Migration Partnership, online).

The distinctions between members of the migrant community are important when considering how they access adult and community learning. For example, individuals seeking asylum are not permitted to work or study until their asylum request has been considered and an outcome reached. This poses some considerable challenges for people integrating successfully into new communities, not least because of the difficulties of accessing English language classes. One of the major lifelong learning programmes which such communities access are English speakers of other languages (ESOL). These programmes are offered by all strands of the lifelong learning sector. However, this sector work hard to access project funding to enable all migrant communities to access ESOL-type programmes: some that enable participants to develop an understanding of the culture of the UK while learning the language; some to develop confidence and competence to speak and listen to spoken English; and others that lead towards a qualification that can verify an individual's English skills which can, in some instances, be used to support asylum-seeker applications or refugee employment applications.

Adult and community learning: older learners

Age is a social construct which links a chronological number to perceptions of competence and capability. For example, you might think about holidays for the 18–30 age group, with associations of particular types of attitudes and behaviours which are vastly different from the types of holidays offered by Saga for the over 55s. As an outcome of the Inquiry into the Future of Lifelong Learning (Schuller and Watson, 2009) a recommendation was made to reconfigure lifelong learning funding from a pre- and post-compulsory model, to a model that reflects the four different stages of life and possible learning needs.

For example, those aged up to 25 should be considered as a whole, with all members of this group being able to claim access to learning and development as a young person. Learning in the second stage of life (25 to 50) should aim at sustaining productivity and prosperity, while also building strong family lives and personal identify. During the third stage (50 to 75) lifelong learning opportunities should reflect the desire of most people in this phase of life to remain active and engaged, and acknowledge 75 as the normal upper age limit for economic activity. In the fourth stage (75 plus) it is argued that lifelong learning opportunities should be developed to reflect a curricula offer for later life.

The adult and community sector already provide a number of lifelong learning programmes for older learners from 55, with a focus on ensuring that older populations continue to be able to access society's mainstream services. A particular area of focus is the need to ensure that such groups develop digital capability and confidence (Age Concern, 2012) as more and more services are driven by technology – for example, making and booking travel arrangements; communication through social networks, Skype and email; managing finances and banking.

Some examples of project funding to support learning programmes to this societal group include 'oral histories', 'silver surfers' and 'intergeneration learning'. All these projects work with older learners to enable them to continue to learn and engage with other age groups in their communities, sharing their own knowledge and developing new skills along the way.

Adult and community learning: rural lifelong learning

Gray noted that lifelong learning in rural communities was a neglected subject, arguing that 'lifelong learning not only makes a critical contribution to the lives of individuals and social groups living and working in the countryside, but also helps to address significant social, economic and political issues in rural areas' (2002: 3). A decade later, rural communities across the UK are in various stages of transformation. Many communities are experiencing inward migration from urban communities or new communities, especially European migrant communities, who are settling in rural environments. Also, there is evidence of outbound migration by young people and adults who are seeking employment, or where housing has priced them out of settling in rural environments. In addition, the demographic profile of rural communities is changing, with an increasingly ageing population.

In line with the findings of many of those who contributed to *Landscapes of Learning* (Gray, 2002), the main challenges to the provision of lifelong learning to rural communities continues to include: viability in terms of learner numbers; transport; access; availability of qualified tutors; working patterns; and childcare. Other barriers identified by Atkin et al. (2005) include: a lack of awareness of available provision or that provision was free; lack of motivation; and cultural perceptions. Reasons given for the lack of motivation by learners included slow or limited progression and limited employment opportunities in rural areas, leading to a belief that there was no value in up-skilling. Rural communities across all areas of the UK have seen rapid growth in populations (Pateman, 2010). Rural communities, like all other communities, are made up of a wide range of adults, requiring a diverse range of curricula. However, rural learners are arguably disadvantaged because the small population numbers tend to mask 'deprivation' indices favouring urban populations. While the geography of rural areas certainly affects learning provision, the social construction of 'rural' also influences lifelong learning provision.

The link between lifelong learning and rural identity is changing as high-technology industries locate to rural areas of the UK, and this creates demands and challenges for adult and community lifelong learning providers, particularly as they work to ensure that the demands of all members of rural communities are provided for.

A major challenge, facing both providers and rural communities trying to access learning opportunities, is an effective transport infrastructure to enable people to attend learning programmes. This results in the need for flexible provision and a diverse range of delivery options utilising a range of technologies, such as e-learning and distance learning. Accessibility and flexibility are crucial for successful provision. Due to varying shift patterns and seasonal work, provision needs to be at a time and location convenient to the learner, and this could change from week to week. This has been long recognised in an agricultural context, but more recently seasonality is linked to the demands of the tourist industry.

There are many obstacles associated with providing lifelong learning opportunities in rural environments (Gray, 2002), including high set-up costs. Across rural areas of the UK, lifelong learning provision in both the formal and non-formal sectors is extensive, complex, diverse and in a state of constant change, but the adult and community learning strand works closely with rural communities to design appropriate learning services, with effective delivery models.

Stakeholders involved in adult and community learning

Local authorities

You might be surprised to know that local authorities play a role in facilitating lifelong learning provision, but they have traditionally had a role to play in ensuring that learning is provided in the community for which they are responsible. Local authorities have a range of models through which they facilitate this learning: some offer provision directly; others commission and manage provision; while a smaller number 'outsource' all their provision to other, larger, further education providers in their area.

Local Authorities work alongside other lifelong learning providers to ensure that a full and comprehensive range of learning programmes are made available for all members of the community. While local authorities may, in some instances, appear to offer the same or similar programmes to other providers of lifelong learning in the community, one of their key objectives is to ensure that learning opportunities are provided: in densely populated areas; in communities where there are diverse ethnic communities; for people who are living in rural communities and may struggle with transport links; for those who may have a high proportion of older people; and where funding mechanisms make it more challenging for other lifelong learning providers to offer a broad learning curriculum.

Third sector

The 'third sector' is a significant provider of lifelong learning, and particularly adult and community learning opportunities. Previously termed the voluntary sector, it works across a wide range of organisations and constituents across all sectors of society. The third sector is generally regarded as the sector that is most successful at engaging and encouraging all strata[1] of society to engage in learning opportunities, but especially successful in working with those members of society who find themselves on the margins of society. The organisations range in size, purpose and focus, and work at community, local, regional and national levels, drawing on paid staff and volunteers. Their provision is often targeted and specialised, having dedicated members of a team who work with one specific group in society in a holistic manner, with the aim of developing an individual's confidence and self-esteem alongside developing other more tangible skills such as those aimed at employability.

One of the largest charities to offer lifelong learning programmes is the Workers' Education Association (WEA). The WEA was founded by Dr Albert Mansbridge, and they are the UK's largest voluntary sector provider of adult education. The organisation was founded in 1903, to support the educational needs of the working population who could not afford to access further or higher education. More than a century on, they continue to provide courses for all adults while also striving to provide educational opportunities, particularly to adults facing social and economic disadvantage. Their programmes attract learners of all ages, with diverse interests and from all areas of society. As a national charity, they offer learning programmes at local, regional and national levels that respond the community needs, often working in partnership with other local communities and groups.

Non-governmental organisations

National Institute of Adult and Continuing Education

An organisation that should be included in this text, which supports all areas of lifelong learning but who are themselves a charity, is the National Institute of Adult Continuing Education (NIACE). NIACE is a membership and charitable organisation that has been involved in advocating, campaigning, promoting and supporting all aspects of adult education since 1921, when they were known as the British Institute for Adult Education. While they do not directly provide training for the sector, the have a broad remit to promote lifelong learning opportunities for all adults. NIACE works with all stakeholders involved in the development and delivery of lifelong learning programmes, including policymakers, government ministers, providers across all strands of the sector and other stakeholders, to develop increased participation in education and training, particularly for those who do not have easy access because of class, gender, age, race, language and culture, learning difficulties or disabilities, or insufficient financial resources.

NIACE runs a number of high-profile campaigns as part of its work to raise the demand for lifelong learning across England and Wales, working closely with it sister organisations in Scotland (the Scottish Adult Learning Partnership) and Northern Ireland (The Northern Ireland Adult Education Association). One of the major and long-standing campaigns run by NIACE is 'Adult Learners' Week', which aims to celebrate the outstanding learning achievements of the lifelong learning community.

Adult Learners' Week is the UK's largest and longest-running festival of learning, promoting adult learning in all its diversity and inspiring people to discover how learning can change their lives. Adult Learners' Week celebrates all kinds of learners and promotes the benefits of every type of learning. For one week in May providers of lifelong learning across England and Wales, supported by NIACE, provide opportunities for their communities to explore many different kinds of learning, showcasing the programmes they provide. The campaign culminates in a series of regional and national award ceremonies that recognise the achievements of outstanding individuals and inspiring learning projects. The campaign attracts significant media coverage and raises awareness of the benefits of engaging in learning of any kind, at any time of life.

Adult and community learning: funding

Funding for adult and community learning comes from a range of sources. Local authorities receive a budget from central government to deliver programmes. While some of the third sector is able to attract government funding, the majority of funding is sought through project funding. The resultant effect is that much of the funding in short term and temporary. This can have significant consequences for provision: programmes take some time to set up and deliver and often the benefits are lost if no long-term funding mechanisms can be found. This is something you should think about as you consider the role of adult and community learning provision. How valued is such provision by government if long-term funding cannot be established, and how can the types of learners we have discussed above be supported to maintain their integration into society if project funding is time-limited?

However, it is noteworthy that some project funding, provided through government initiatives, have had significantly positive effects on lifelong learning provision, particularly in this strand of the sector. Examples of such projects include the following.

The Transformation Fund

The implementation of the White Paper *The Learning Revolution* (DIUS, 2009) provided a fund – The Transformation Fund – to support a rise both in the profile of adult and community learning, and the uptake of lifelong learning opportunities.

This Fund (2009/2010) was provided at the time of the New Labour government with the ambition of creating new opportunities for people to engage in informal adult and community learning in England. As a result of the Fund, over one million adults were given the chance to participate in lifelong learning. The Transformation Fund formed part of a commitment by the Labour government, outlined in the Learning Revolution White Paper (DIUS, 2008), to provide a new way of improving people's lives and prosperity through 'learning for pleasure' (this term is an alternative to explain informal learning – learning that is non-accredited). The government provided £20 million to support the Transformation Fund project. The objective for the Fund was to enable creative learning to flourish across the country, and the projects that ran as part of it introduced a range of innovative adult learning initiatives that benefited both communities and individuals. As a result of the project many people from a range of backgrounds, and particularly people from disadvantaged groups, were able to access learning in new places, in new ways and at more flexible times. Importantly, some projects enabled people to establish their own self-organised groups and learning clubs, facilitated through the funding and adult and community learning providers. NIACE was contracted to mange this fund on behalf of the government.

Funding context

Following the publication, in December 2011, of *New Challenges, New Chances: Further Education and Skills System Reform Plan: Building a World Class Skills System* (DBIS, 2011b), a pilot scheme was launched by the DBIS in April 2012 – Community Learning Trust Pilots. In the ministerial forward, John Hayes, the Minister of State for Further Education, Skills and Lifelong Learning, acknowledges that 'learning is precious because it brings light to all kinds of lives' (DBIS, 2012: 3), recognising that 'accessible community learning is an indispensable feature of any learning and skills system that truly claims to be lifelong' (DBIS, 2012: 3).

In this document there is a suggestion that community learning should offer a sense of personal fulfilment, but also should work to break down barriers which appear to divide communities, and also has a role in the development of neighbourhoods that feel secure and welcoming. As well as supporting the social aspect of learning, there is an implicit recognition in the document that engagement in this type of learning can contribute to the growth of local economies, as evidence suggests that as people engage in learning and develop their skills, confidence and independence they feel able to progress to training and employment. Importantly, this type of community learning may or may not lead to a qualification, but it has the potential to be transformative in terms of developing people in both tangible and intangible ways.

However, there is a recognition that community learning opportunities are very often vulnerable during periods of economic fragility, and so it seems that this type of learning often needs to be 'championed' or defended in some way, as it becomes vulnerable to increasing marginalisation or cuts. In this new pilot model, presented in April 2012, it is argued that learning is 'not just for local people and their communities, but rather belongs to local people and must answer to them' (DBIS, 2012: 3).

Community Learning Trusts

This fund has been newly introduced by the Coalition government (2012). The ambition of this funding to is pilot local Community Learning Trusts as a model to test new ways of delivering community learning. The pilot aims to run from August 2012, with partnerships made up of community learning providers and other local organisations working together to increase local decision making about local learning priorities, and to develop financial models that will enable community learning to continue to grow and flourish. It is expected that the Trusts will also focus on delivering the new community learning objectives outlined in *New Challenges, New Chances* (DBIS, 2011b), which included increasing participation in lifelong learning and providing a forum where local people have a voice in decisions about adult learning in their communities. Each Trust will explore ways which in people can be encouraged and motivated to access learning programmes, particularly disadvantaged group or rural communities.

Again, NIACE have been contracted to manage these Trusts on behalf of the government, which will operate for one year. The findings of this project will inform the funding and delivery of lifelong learning for the adult and community learning strand of the lifelong learning sector going forward.

This is an interesting perspective and provides some interesting and challenging dilemmas. Over recent decades funding for community learning has been centralised and 'ring fenced', meaning that central organisations working to government agendas have guided the type of learning that could be provided by such organisations. For example, if an individual was interested in learning about digital photography they may be invited to enrol for a literacy class which would be delivered within the context of digital photography but may have additional requirements attached to it, such as the students being required to undertake a literacy assessment.

This new model of community learning suggests that actually the people within a community will decide on the learning offer – the curriculum – and be accountable for its success or otherwise. This raises questions about whether local communities feel able or confident to decide what the community needs to learn, how that information is gathered and then what is done with that information. Arguably, these are the very areas that have driven the community learning offer to date. The community pilots are being run during 2012 and it will be interesting to read their results.

Summary

A major ambition for adult and community learning is to focus on the creation of a cohesive community by encouraging and motivating a culture in learning. That results in active, engaged, socially responsible citizens and also, perhaps as an unintended consequence, raises the ability of individuals to be more economically effective and engaged. This ambition aligns with many government agendas that have generally focused on models of social justice – moving from social exclusion, to inclusion, to social justice – and spans many aspects of current government policy under the umbrella of the Big Society.

One of key characteristics of this strand of learning is its focus on informal learning – that is, learning that does not generally lead to a qualification outcome, but builds an individual's self-esteem and confidence so that they can progress into other strands of the sector, such as further education or work-based learning opportunities. Most often this sector will be working with groups of learners who are traditionally considered to be 'hard to reach' – who are often identified as being socially or economically disadvantaged. Some of these groups have been outlined above.

The funding for this sector is by no means stable. It is often reliant on project funding, and this is perhaps the biggest challenge for providers of lifelong learning who wish to develop programmes that have the duration to support individuals to a point where they have the confidence and capability to move to other types of provision.

4

Higher education

This chapter will discuss the role of higher education within a lifelong learning framework. The aim of the chapter is to enable you to develop a critical understanding of the purpose of higher education for contemporary UK society, focusing particularly on lifelong learning and widening participation. Three questions have been developed to facilitate this discussion.

Firstly, the chapter will consider the question: what is higher education? This allows us to explore how higher education was established, and then track its evolution. Importantly, this question will consider what members of UK society have traditionally accessed higher education, and why? What did access to higher education enable people to achieve? And what were the consequences of not accessing higher education for other members of society? To enable us to answer these questions we will need to consider some of the key policy decisions that have been made and some of the key sociological reasons given for the establishment of higher education in the UK, particularly concepts such as cultural reproduction and capital: social, economic and cultural.

The second question I want to explore as we continue to think about the role of lifelong learning in the contemporary UK is the notion of widening participation in higher education, asking the question: what is meant by widening participation in higher education? This is a key area of focus for the development of higher education and I want to explore the notion of widening participation: what members of society are being invited to participate in higher education and why? What is the influence of holding a higher education qualification on social and economic opportunities? Is the rise in numbers of people accessing and experiencing higher education influencing the structure of society? Here we will pay particular attention to exploring the policies that have established and continue to influence widening participation, and consider the concept of social mobility.

The third question I want to consider is: who is under-participating in higher education and why? This question enables us to explore, using a different perspective, why some members of society access higher education and others do not. This discussion will focus on how higher education policy either enables individuals to access higher education or actually acts as a barrier to accessing higher education, inhibiting or preventing the potential for social mobility or capital – social, economic or cultural.

By the end of this chapter, you will have gained a critical understanding of the role of higher education in supporting lifelong learning opportunities, and be able to question how our society has established mechanisms to maintain our social structures and worked to ensure progression and development for a more equal society through widening participation strategies. You will be able to locate these discussions within a framework of social mobility, drawing on the theoretical framework of 'capitals' adopted by Bourdieu to explore models of social reproduction.

Task

Take a minute to consider the following questions:

- What do you think higher education is for?
- Should everyone really be able to access higher education? Why?

Jot down a couple of ideas about why you decided to undertake a higher education qualification and why.

What is higher education?

Higher education is a well-established strand of education across the developed and developing world. The original concept behind the creation of universities is identified by Bauman (1997: 17) as 'the gathering of teachers and students in pursuit of the higher learning', and so ancient centres for higher learning were established. Across the United Kingdom, all four countries have a well-established tradition of offering higher education opportunities to their population. In England, Oxford University was established in 1167 and Cambridge not long after in 1209; in Scotland, St Andrews was founded in 1413; in Northern Ireland Queen's University of Belfast was chartered in 1845 and in Wales, the University of Aberystwyth was established in 1872. The main areas and focus of study for students at this time included philosophy, ancient history and religion.

Following the creation of these first universities, a tradition was established that universities were shaped in order to enable the transmission of higher knowledge from one generation to the next. The areas of knowledge studied were largely theoretical rather than pragmatic, with students who engaged in such pursuits mainly drawn from the higher echelons of society.

Higher education as a mechanism for cultural reproduction

Universities could be considered to be instruments of 'cultural reproduction', perpetuating and maintaining an established social hierarchy in our society by facilitating the distribution of professional careers among its graduates. 'Cultural reproduction' is a term used to explain how 'culture' is passed on from one generation to another. The word 'culture' describes the norms and values associated with a particular group or society, and how these transfer between societies, subgroups within a society and also between individuals. Bourdieu's work on education and social reproduction (Bourdieu and Passeron, 1977) provides a useful explanation, and way of understanding how the positions of people in a society are constructed and continuously maintained by the dominant few upon the dominated majority, through influences of family, of community and, particularly, of education.

Task

Take a minute to think about what 'culture' might mean for you. Do you use particular speech phrases that your parents have used; do you have a meal at a particular time because that is 'traditional' in your family; do you practice a particular religion or faith because that is part of your community; do you have particular festivals that you celebrate as part of your culture; are you studying at a particular university, or a particular course because that is the tradition of your family? These are examples of cultural norms – and you will probably be able to think of many more.

The role of lifelong learning in the development of society

As we saw in Chapter 1, education is a key institution through which cultural norms and values can be shared and passed on from one generation to another in a particular society. This practice is explored through a range of sociological models, the most notable of which include functionalism, structuralism and social interactionism. The work of Giddens (2007) provides a very clear introduction into some of the key sociological thinking and developments that have informed, and continue to influence, the way our contemporary UK society has evolved and developed culturally. It is important to have a clear understand of these models as they influence the purpose and focus of higher education and importantly lifelong learning, as outlined below.

The role of lifelong learning for society from a functionalist perspective

Functionalism is a sociological model which argues that people are born into a particular position in society, and that all members of society agree that the position should be maintained. In order for each member of society to recognise their position, they are 'educated' to take up that place – so their educational experience reflects their predetermined place in society. This approach to societal constructs is often referred to as a 'consensus' approach.

Influential thinkers who developed this sociological model include Parsons (1961) and Durkheim (1982). Functionalists assert that the purpose of education is to prepare young people to take up their allocated role in society, which is reflective of the position in society into which they were born, and to teach them the basic skills they will need for the type of job they are likely to achieve. Additionally, education, using this model, is expected to teach young people the rules and values of the subgroup of society which they inhabit.

However, functionalists also believe that a person can change their position in society based on their merit – known as meritocracy – meaning that all members of society have access to education and 'the more you put in, the more you get out'. Functionalists argue that, regardless of your background, gender, ethnicity, race or class, you will attain your rightful position in society based on your own commitment to hard work.

The role of lifelong learning for society from a structuralist perspective

As a response to the functionalist perspective, an alternative model to the purpose of education is the structuralist approach. This approach is often referred to as a 'conflict' model and incorporates a Marxist response to education. This model sees society as being made up of groups, or subgroups, that are competing for a place in society. They argue that education acts to reproduce inequalities that exist in society by controlling the education provided. This control can be seen, for example, by the type of resources provided to education by the state and also by controlling what is being taught through, for example, a national curriculum. A key sociological thinker in this perspective is Althusser (see Giddens, 2007).

Both of these approaches to considering the role of education in society explore education as a major institution nationally, adopting a macro (whole/big) view of society.

The role of lifelong learning for society from a social interactionist perspective

Contrastingly, social interactionists explore the role of education from a micro (small) perspective, looking at the relationships between the structure – institution of education – and the role of the individuals who access it, which is often referred to as the 'structure–agency' debate. This model explores how individuals navigate institutions (in this case education) to influence and potentially transform society. A key thinker in this perspective is Willis (1977), who explored the interactions that took place in the classroom between teachers and students ,and also between peer groups, to develop and establish cultural norms and behaviours.

Lifelong learning and cultural reproduction

For some, such as Bourdieu (1977, 1997 and 1998), cultural reproduction is identified as the key mechanism through which a social hierarchy, or social order, is maintained in a society, which enables certain privileges to be maintained by specific sectors of society through the institutional mechanism of education. On this view, higher education in particular works to effect cultural reproduction.

Lifelong learning aims work within such established sociological models to develop opportunities for people to expand their accepted cultural norms and values beyond established boundaries and social hierarchies. It is also important for you to be able to distinguish between social, economic and cultural capitals, as these terms are often used to explain the benefits of engagement in lifelong learning generally, and are particularly important when considering why people engage in higher education.

Understanding higher education through a 'capitals' framework

The term 'capital' is often used when talking about the value, or otherwise, of a particular educational experience. One of the most highly regarded writers of recent times, who has drawn on this concept to explore education, is Bourdieu (1977), who uses the term 'capital' particularly to refer to different types of power. He asserts that sets of constraints, or capitals, are inscribed in a society and govern how it – the society – functions. Three distinct forms of capital are identified by Bourdieu (1993, 1997) that influence the (re)production of a society. These are: social capital, which is made up of social obligations or 'connections' that are convertible, in certain conditions, into economic capital; economic capital, which is immediately and directly convertible into money; and cultural capital, which is convertible in certain conditions into economic capital.

It is important to recognise that these three forms of capital have independence and distinction, as well as an interplay and potential conversion between them.

Social capital

For some, engaging in a higher education experience is part of the 'norm': it is what their circle of friends is doing, and what their parent and extended family have done. For those who are the target of the widening participation agenda, higher education is not part of their social network experience and therefore, arguably, does not form part of their normal possibilities. Social capital is nicely explained by Field (2003: 1) as 'relationships matter'. The concept broadly refers to the access people have to varying stocks of an asset not resting in their pockets (Putnam, 2000). While for some, social capital is seen as a positive way of thinking about social interactions, for others, such as Bourdieu (1977) it is regarded as a concept which reflects a mechanism of social control within established structured systems of social positions, with relationships between people being constructed by domination, subordination or equivalency.

Economic capital

Economic capital is identified by Bourdieu as the most powerful form of capital that acts to overarch and influence all aspects of social reproduction, and particularly cultural and social capital. Bourdieu explains economic capital as:

> at the root of all the other types of capital and that these transformed, disguised forms of economic capital, never entirely reducible to that definition, produce their most specific effects only to the extent that they conceal (not least from their possessors) the fact that economic capital is at their root.
>
> (Bourdieu, 1997: 53)

Economic capital can also be discussed in terms of 'human capital', which refers to the number of people in a community who have the capacity to work at particular levels of employment and that have an economic return for the country. Financial limitations or restrictions often make higher education unaffordable or inaccessible. While many strategies, as part of the overall widening participation strategy, have been put in place over recent decades to more readily enable engagement in higher education, there continues to be an inevitable short-term cost associated with higher education – in the form of loss of earnings. While the research clearly demonstrates a strong link between higher earning capacity and those who hold a degree, for some potential students the short-term loss of earning and the longer-term associated debt results in an imbalance of economic capital.

Cultural capital

For some people there is a lack of connection with what might be possible. Cultural capital is a term used to explain that which is accumulated over time and often handed down from generation to generation in terms of expectations, norms, values and beliefs. Cultural capital was used by Bourdieu to consider the unequal academic achievements of individuals in the education system and how the distribution of 'cultural capital' was invested, with the resultant effects on academic success measured through qualification outcome.

Cultural capital particularly informed his work in considering how social groups attribute value to learning and its consequential influence upon social reproduction, noting that as a result of the unequal distribution of cultural capital it can become a marker of distinction and social privilege (Webb, et al., 2002). For those who are the potential targets of the widening participation agenda, they could be considered as unable to make a connection between what has been possible and achievable within their known experiences and the potential outside of their known experiences.

So capitals, according to Bourdieu, can be used both to explain and understand how a society functions as it constructs societal norms, rules and regulations. It is important to be aware that capitals can be accumulated, lost, invested, distributed and traded across social spaces or social strata, and can explain how individuals come to be positioned in society. Capitals are useful to bear in mind when considering how individuals have traditionally accessed higher education, and how the widening participation agenda has worked to influence individuals' access to higher education.

Reflection

Having read the above explanations for the possible role of education, and higher education particularly, do you think that your experience of education as a young person allowed you to achieve to your potential, or do you think your potential was limited either by your environment, your peers, your teachers or your institution?

Would you say that you were educated to take a particular role in society (a functionalist approach)? Do you think that you were given every opportunity to be the best that you could be regardless of who you are – regardless, for example, of your gender, the colour of your skin, the area in which you live, or how well your siblings achieved (a conflict approach)?

Take a minute to think about the interactions you engaged in during your previous experiences of education. Do you think that your teacher built a relationship with you based on your background? When you sought information about future career options or further study were you advised to revise your ambitions, or guided towards particular types of employment (social interactionist approach)?

By answering the above question, you will be able to develop a critical understanding of what the role of higher education is in our contemporary society. Once you have established why you think higher education exists, we now need to think about the role of lifelong learning for higher education through the widening participation agenda.

Widening participation in higher education

Often, when people think about lifelong learning, there is a determined focus on lower levels of learning, initial basic skills learning, or learning to enable those who have become marginalised from society to reintegrate into mainstream society and gain equal access to all the services and resources available within it. However, within the social justice framework of lifelong learning, it is important to think about lifelong learning and its potential to influence all aspects of an individual's life to reach their potential.

Research shows us that in contemporary UK society the higher the level of qualification an individual achieves, the higher the potential earning income that can be achieved, which, in turn, can have positive consequential influences on life prospects – socially and economically as well as culturally. We have seen in the above discussions how higher education has arguably been used to ensure that the culture of our society, and the social privileges that this implies, is reproduced. However, economic opportunities are one of the major reasons why people today study for a degree, which has associations of status within our society – and inevitably power.

Task

Take a minute to make a note of the distinguishing features of each of these capitals and what these might mean for lifelong learning and widening participation in higher education.

Further reading on the work of Bourdieu will help you to understand the relationship between capitals. A good introductory text to his work is provided by Richard Jenkins (2002).

Access to higher education

Access to higher education has often been limited to members of society who could be considered 'higher class' or more privileged. Lifelong learning for higher education supports an opening up of access to higher education, supporting the development of a broad range of widening participation strategies, policies and interventions.

The aim of this programme of activity was established, ambitiously some might say, to provide society with more equal opportunities to achieve social mobility and progression by accessing and achieving higher education qualifications, and enabling increased social, economic and cultural capital. These areas are the focus for discussion in this section, which will explore lifelong learning within the context of widening participation in higher education, focusing on the role of lifelong learning in crafting and supporting the participation of non-traditional students into higher education.

The questions that we explore here include: how much, if anything, has changed since the original inception of higher education institutions? What has been the role of lifelong learning, and particularly the widening participation agenda, in contributing to the development and purpose of higher education in the contemporary UK? What has been the impact of lifelong learning on access to higher education and how it has influenced social mobility, if at all?

Task

Before we discuss the widening participation agenda, take a few minutes to think about whether you could consider yourself a beneficiary of this agenda by answering the following questions:

1. How did you get to university? What qualifications did you study? Did you get any help with your university application? Who from?
2. How did you choose this course? Why?
3. How did you choose this university? Why?
4. Are you the first in your family to go to university?
5. Did you have a role model who encouraged you to attend university? Who was it?
6. What do you plan to do as a result of achieving your degree?

Think about your answers to these questions as we consider the rise of the widening participation agenda for higher education in the contemporary UK.

The historical policy of widening participation in higher education

Widening participation is a term used to discuss, and address, the under-representation in higher education of all members of society, with a particular focus on individuals from lower socio-economic groups.

Robbins Report (1963): Committee on Higher Education

In 1961 the government commissioned a Committee on Higher Education, chaired by Lord Robbins, to explore the role of higher education for England going forward. The committee met from 1961 to 1963, after which they published their report. The *Robbins Report* (Committee on Higher Education, 1963) is regarded as a significant and influential report that was instrumental in the transformation of higher education, particularly its role in supporting lifelong learning by recommending widening access to, and participation in, higher education for more of the UK population. The report was the result of a long inquiry into the role of higher education in the UK in which four key principles were identified that higher education should focus on providing:

1. Instruction in skills for employment;
2. Promoting the general powers of the mind;

3. Advancing learning; and

4. Transmission of a common culture and common standard of citizenship.

These recommendations were accepted by the government in 1963. In order to achieve these ambitions, an expansion of public sector higher education in the form of polytechnics was agreed. This was initially achieved by giving existing 'colleges of advanced technology' university status. However, the authors of the report agreed that the growth in higher educational opportunities should continue to ensure that university places be made available to all those who were qualified to access them based on ability and attainment. It is interesting to note here the continued focus on cultural reproduction and an ambition to achieve a common understanding of citizenship.

Following the *Robbins Report*, many polytechnics were established alongside universities. Polytechnics were regarded as tertiary education (following compulsory and further education) teaching institutions that offered undergraduate-level qualifications in a range of areas that most often resulted in a vocational outcome (for example in engineering or design), whereas traditional universities continued to offer a more traditional range of programmes that were regarded as more academic and less associated with employment opportunities (for example philosophy, history and geography). This distinction between the curricula offered to students led to what became known as a 'binary divide', with significant differentiation being made between the value of 'vocational' polytechnic qualifications and 'academic' university qualifications between 1965 and 1992. This was mainly because polytechnics did not have degree-awarding powers.

On reflection, polytechnics were seen to focus on applied education for work – as institutions there was less focus on undertaking research and many of their programmes required lower qualifications for entry than more traditional universities. The result of this distinction between universities and polytechnics resulted in a societal perception of polytechnics being inferior in status to universities, affirming cultural reproduction rather that opening opportunities for all members of society to access higher education and thereby widen participation.

Widening participation: the creation of the Open University

A significant outcome of these ambitions to broaden the higher education system, and enable all members of society to access this level of qualification, was the creation of the Open University. Instrumental in the foundation of the Open University was the leader of the Labour party in the 1960s, Harold Wilson. Following his election to power in 1964, he appointed Jennie Lee to the post of Minister of Arts and asked her to take over the 'University of the Air' project (the first name given to the Open University, which reflected the ambition to have a higher education institution that was available to all through the medium of the airwaves (radio technology)).

Following their successful re-election in 1967, a planning committee was established to develop a comprehensive plan for an 'open university'. The first Vice Chancellor for the Open University was appointed in 1969, and the first university students were recruited in 1971. The Open University had, and continues to have, a quite radical open admissions policy, with no requirement for any prior educational qualifications to be achieved before starting a programme of study. The Open University became a world-class and very successful distance teaching university, breaking the link between higher education access and exclusivity and playing a major role in providing opportunities for widening participation in higher education.

However, arguably the system became distorted. There was evidence of a need to revisit the development of access to higher education, particularly in light of global changes and demands on the economy – not least the recognition of a need to have a greater degree of the population with the necessary skills to meet the challenges of new emerging employment markets that demanded higher-level skills and capabilities.

The policy of widening participation in higher education: 1990–2000

Under the leadership of the Conservative Prime Minister, John Major, a new philosophy of education (a functionalist consensual approach) was adopted which ended the two-tier system between universities and polytechnics that was regarded by many as confusing. This was achieved through the implementation of the 1992 *Further and Higher Education Act* (Great Britain, 1992), which ensured that polytechnics were re-established as universities, so creating one unified system of higher education aimed at developing modern universities that could support student numbers and respond to the emerging global economic demands.

The *Dearing Report* (1997): the United Kingdom National Committee of Inquiry to Higher Education

The election of the New Labour government in 1997 saw the establishment of the United Kingdom National Committee of Inquiry to Higher Education. The Committee was tasked with reviewing the aims, purposes and role of higher education for the next 20 years. The committee, chaired by Lord Dearing, reported in 1997. In their conclusions they made it very clear that universities should be responsible for the promotion of a learning society by making lifelong learning one of the purposes of higher education. You can see here the ambition of developing a culture of learning that we discussed in earlier chapters.

The *Dearing Report* (1997) reviewed, refreshed and extended the previous aims outlined by the *Robbins Report* (Committee on Higher Education, 1963) and built on them. The focus for higher education for the future, according to the *Dearing Report* should be:

1. Imparting employment skills;
2. Providing opportunities for adult lifelong learning to enable individuals, employers and the nation to adapt to changing circumstances;
3. Promoting the general powers of the mind;
4. Advancing learning and research;
5. Promoting culture and high standards in all aspects of society; and
6. Serving local regional communities and national interests at home and abroad.

You can see here how the committee continues to refer to the importance of cultural reproduction, but also had a strong focus on a more accessible system that enabled a broader range of the population to be able to access, and engage in, higher education. The *Dearing Report* argued that lifelong learning was a culture and should incorporate self-directed learning, credit accumulation, access and continuing professional development, as well as distance and open learning (Bill, 1998), and should be the focus of higher education provision going forward in order that everyone can access and use the information necessary for future engagement in society – socially, economically and culturally.

Learning Works: Widening Participation in Further Education (1997)

A seminal report by Helena Kennedy was also published in 1997: *Learning Works* argued favourably for the widening of access to higher education for society. While the committee was tasked, working under the chairmanship of Kennedy, with examining participation in further education (explored in the next chapter), in spending some time reviewing the evolution of the further education sector they concluded there was a need to both widen participation in learning as well as increase participation. This is a subtle but important distinction which arose from their work, which identified that changes in funding mechanisms, as well as the increased marketisation of learning (making learning a commodity for sale), had potentially led to the exclusion of some sectors of society from learning opportunities, particularly members of lower socio-economic groups.

Consequences of the Dearing Report (1997) and Kennedy (1997)

As a result of both the *Dearing Report* and Kennedy's *Learning Works* report, a series of recommendations were made regarding widening access to, and participation in, higher education. It is important to record that government accepted all 93 of the recommendations made in the *Dearing Report* (1997). Examples of recommendations made by the Committee to widen participation, which include short-, medium- and long-term recommendations and were based on the principles outlined above, included:

1. As part of the development of a long-term strategy to respond to the increasing demands for higher education, at degree and sub-degree level, government should remove the capping of numbers of undergraduates securing places at universities. (Funding for university will be explored later in this chapter but it is noteworthy that numbers of students who can access higher education are limited as a result of government funding for higher education.)

2. The expansion of higher education provision should be supported by increased funding, being directed to higher education providers who are able to demonstrate a commitment to widening participation through the development of a widening participation strategy for their institution which had monitoring mechanisms attached to it.

3. Funding should be provided to institutions to enable learning support for students with disabilities, and extend the scope of the Disabled Students' Allowance.

4. A framework for data about lifelong learning should be developed, using a unique student record number to be created by stakeholders involved in the delivery of higher education.

Reflection

The recommendations outlined above are only a few examples. Take a few minutes to look up the *Dearing Report* for yourself online and record how many of the recommendations were linked to funding and how many, you think, were actually implemented. For example, there was a recommendation that students should be allowed to access social security benefits (chapter 7, recommendation 5) which was not realised. Can you identify any others? Which particular recommendations focused on lifelong learning?

Strategies and interventions to support widening participation

There are a range of strategies and interventions that have been developed to support the widening participation agenda in the UK since the Dearing and Kennedy Reports. Some of these include:

The Sutton Trust

The Sutton Trust is a charitable foundation that was established in 1997 to support and promote social mobility in society through education. The Trust works with all sectors of education, from primary stages through to university, to develop access opportunities for individuals to all aspects of education. The Trust aims to eradicate inequalities in education opportunities and provision, and support the development of an educational system that allows individuals to excel regardless of their demographic location in society, securing positions in the highest quality higher education providers.

Aimhigher

This initiative was established by government to encourage young people to progress their education into higher education. The programme developed a range of initiatives and activities aimed at motivating and supporting learners, particularly from lower socio-economic groups and disadvantaged backgrounds living in deprived areas, to enter higher education but who may be lacking in confidence or felt they were underachieving. Aimhigher was seen as the major vehicle for widening access to higher education during the governance of the New Labour government. Funding for this programme came to an end in 2011, following the election of the Liberal Democrat–Conservative Coalition government in 2010.

Widening Participation Strategy

In 2003, the UK government developed a *Widening Participation Strategy* (DfES, 2003e) which created a framework for the future development of widening participation for higher education providers to work within to support individuals in accessing higher education. The framework used four areas of focus: attainment, aspiration, application and admissions, ensuring that higher education providers were transparent in the systems they used to enable individuals to access their programmes and that students were supported to attain to the best of their potential.

Office for Fair Access (OFFA)

One of the main mechanisms used to ensure the establishment of a strong widening participation agenda was the creation of the OFFA, which was established as part of the 2004 Higher Education Act as a non-department public body to work with higher education institutions to enable them to manage the introduction of tuition fees. It ensured that there was no detrimental effect on the ambitions for the widening participation agenda, supporting higher education providers to develop financial support packages and bursaries for those from lower-income backgrounds and other under-represented groups.

Higher education providers are required to develop access agreements that are submitted to the OFFA for approval if they wish to charge tuition fees above basic levels. The OFFA monitors these agreements to ensure access agreements are adhered to.

Reflection

These are only a few examples of strategies and interventions that were developed during the first decade of the millennium to support widening participation in higher education.

Take a few minutes to see if you can source further strategies.

Do you think you were supported to access higher education as a result of a widening participation intervention?

Also, do you think that these strategies have been successful in achieving their ambitions to enable social mobility through access to higher education?

Summary of policy developments

We have spent some time thinking about what higher education is, and what widening participation means both for society, and higher education in contemporary society. We have considered how education is established as an influential institution in informing cultural reproduction, which can be usefully explained and considered using different types of capital – social, economic and cultural. Particularly, we have considered how widening participation strategies have worked to overcome some of the embedded social structures to provide opportunities for social mobility, and considered how this agenda has focused particularly on enabling upward social mobility for groups from lower socio-economic groups, from disadvantaged backgrounds and deprived communities. Before we go on to consider who is actually under-represented in higher education, it is necessary to ensure that you have an understanding of the concept of social mobility.

Lifelong learning, higher education and social mobility

In its simplest form, social mobility refers to the movement of individuals or groups to different social positions. Most often social mobility is considered in economic terms and you could be considered to have increased your social status if you increase your income, and so is often considers a positive upward vertical mobility. Access to higher education, arguably, affords the opportunity to gain higher qualifications and higher-status employment with higher earning potential, perhaps leading to an increase in social class and enabling social mobility. However, it is important to recognise that social mobility can refer to moving across social levels horizontally, and can also be negatively vertical. An increase in equality of opportunity in a society is most often noted as a result of intergenerational mobility, where there is evidence of a positive change in status between an individual and their parents or previous family generations. Social mobility is influenced by the 'capitals' discussed previously.

Underparticipating in higher education

Task

Before we consider why certain groups may be under-represented, or under-participating in higher education, consider the following question: what might be the barriers to participation in higher education?

There are generally two major agendas associated with attending university: a government one and a personal one.

From a government perspective there is a long-term desire to support people to access and obtain a higher level of education. Having a high percentage of the population who have a higher level of education affords the opportunity for a higher level of employment, particularly in areas of science, technology, engineering and mathematics (STEM), and creates a 'human capital' stock (look back at the section on economic capital earlier in this chapter to refresh your memory of what this means).

From an individual perspective, many young people attend university following completion of their Level 3 studies as part of their 'natural progression'. It is part of their cultural 'norm' to go on to university to study at this level. Some people consider going into higher education as a response to redundancy, in order to upgrade their employment or career opportunities, recognising that this is likely to require a higher level of education, and have a very economic-driven perspective on the value of a higher education experience. Others attend higher education as a 'returner' – people who, for whatever reason, have not engaged in their initial compulsory education, or found it to be a very negative experience, and have decided to return to education as a mature student to undertake higher education for personal fulfilment, reflective of a social capital approach to the value of education.

A significant force behind the widening participation strategy (DfES, 2003e) was to encourage those from non-traditional backgrounds or with non-traditional qualification to access university programmes. Examples of such groups notably include people with learning difficulties or disabilities and black and minority ethnic communities. A non-traditional higher education learner can be explained through the framework of social class or social hierarchy.

Social hierarchy

Social hierarchy is an established system – often referred to as a class system, or a social order. In the UK the system of social class is a well-established system through which people are located in a particular position in society. It is an example of a stratification system that is widely used in the UK to explain the way in which our society functions. The system was historically aligned to a man's occupational status, and is closely associated with wealth and power.

The social class model used widely in the UK today, for example when collecting national statistics, is based on a three-tier system of class – upper, middle and lower classes. More recently however, additional strata, or sub-divisions, have been created, for example: underclass, upper working class, lower middle class. This evolution aims to reflect the broad range of people and occupations. The additional layers have been added to the system as a result of many more people having access to a greater range of educational opportunities, making movement between the classes' strata easier because of occupational achievement – social mobility. Importantly, however, an underclass has also evolved which focuses on groups of the population who have limited, if any, educational qualifications, often becoming long-term unemployed as they struggle to gain employment in a society which has moved from an economy based on manufacturing to one that is now based on knowledge. The concept of a knowledge society is explored in Chapter 1.

There are a variety of models and reasons that have been developed to explain why people do not engage in higher education, which include:

Situational awareness

The reality of some people's lives means that they are unaware that it may be possible for them to engage in higher education. The Aimhigher project works with such groups to demonstrate that higher education is a reasonable ambition and aspiration for all members of society.

Learning disposition

In reality, for some there is little motivation or attraction to engage in higher learning opportunities. Some groups do not see the potential benefits of achieving a higher education qualification, either socially, culturally or (in particular) economically. A major barrier to engaging in learning is often financial.

Despite the efforts of government, through a range of widening participation strategies, it is apparent that non-traditional students continue to be less likely to engage in higher education, and if they do that they are less likely to access universities that have higher positions within the hierarchy of higher education institutions. It is important to understand what might be considered the 'push–pull' factors that influence an individual's decision, whether conscious or subconscious, to engage in higher education. This is particularly important as we consider the development of higher education resulting from the election of the Liberal Democrat–Conservative Coalition government in 2010, and the importance of the development of a fair and equal society.

Higher education going forward: *The Browne Report* (2010)

Higher Education in the United Kingdom is undergoing a period of significant change, which is the culmination of a series of factors.

Firstly, during 2009 the then New Labour government commissioned Lord Browne to chair a committee to review the funding of and for higher education. This committee was set to report in 2010. However, during this period the Conservative and Liberal Democrat parties were voted into power and formed a joint Coalition government in May 2010.

This is important for several reasons. Firstly, each political party has very different views and ideas about the role of higher education, its funding and who should be able to access it. Importantly, when the New Labour government commissioned the Browne review in 2009, both these parties were opposed to the review, but for very different reasons. Following their election in May 2010, however, and upon publication of the Browne Report in November 2010, the Coalition government accepted many of the recommendations made in the *Browne Report* (Browne, 2010). The report received a very strong and heated response, not only from political parties but also from higher education institutions and students accessing higher education.

The *Browne Report* (2010) made a number of wide-ranging proposals on reform to the current system of higher education funding based on the following principles:

- That all those who can benefit from higher education are able to do so, regardless of financial circumstances;
- Increasing investment for higher education;
- Increasing student choice;
- That government should meet the upfront costs of education;
- That loans should be repaid on a income-contingent basis; and
- Increasing support for part-time students.

The most significant and fundamental recommendation made by the report was the removal of the established capped charges for tuition fees, enabling higher education providers to raise their fees to a maximum of £9,000 per academic year. This and other financial changes to the funding of higher education, creating competition between universities, caused some concern for the continuing commitment to widening participation.

However, as part of the new model of higher education, it is expected that government will impose a regime in English universities which will deny them the right to charge tuition fees if they fail to admit sufficient numbers of students from disadvantaged backgrounds. This mechanism will be driven through the OFFA (see above for explanation of their purpose) via access agreements built by universities. While many universities are hoping to increase tuition fees in line with Browne's recommendations, if they want to charge more that £6,000 they will have to find a way to attract many more students from disadvantaged backgrounds onto their courses. The OFFA will have a significant set of powers to ensure institutions meet their commitments to improve social mobility.

Task

Go online and download the executive summary of the *Browne Report* and review the recommendations made for the future of higher education provision in contemporary UK.

So, what is a modern university? Higher education today is both responsible for and responsive to widening access to the information revolution. It can be considered to be a 'massified' system for the up-skilling of the general population – creating a commodification of the individual (human capital). Higher education is now intimately integrated with, and responsive to, commercial needs, while also being situated within and responsive to local community needs and demands. Importantly, a modern university should be working to draw its students from all groups in society. Universities today are seen as a major facilitator of employability and also as a means to redress social inequity. The question for us to consider is whether this is a reality for modern-day universities as higher education becomes a much more competitive, market-driven environment. Do universities continue to be committed to a widening participation agenda or have we reverted to a system based on individual meritocracy and privilege?

The future of higher education is uncertain and changing. It is unclear at the time of writing what the impact of the reforms to higher education will have – for higher education as an institution, as a mechanism for widening participation and within a framework of lifelong learning. Areas for interest will include: whether the opportunity for students to have access to funding for part-time study will result in more students opting to study part-time while working; whether there will be diversity in the type and range of programmes made available through higher education; and what delivery models will best suit a learning society of the future. Of particular interest will be the engagement and participation of students: will they change as the funding mechanisms change? A particular concern here in terms of the widening participation agenda is whether those who are considered to be non-traditional learners may be more reticent and concerned about acquiring some level of debt prior to commencing employment.

Reflection

In light of the above discussions, consider the following questions:

1. Are the strategies put in place to enable those from disadvantaged backgrounds to access higher education realistic? Do they work? What is the evidence?
2. Why should we widen participation to higher education when the system is currently oversubscribed?
3. Should access to higher education be based on merit and successful academic achievement alone?
4. Is higher education, as part of lifelong learning, really a mechanism for social mobility?

Summary

This chapter has introduced you to higher education as a part of the lifelong learning framework. It has provided a brief outline and introduction to higher education in England, and then considered issues around widening participation for lifelong learning. We started with the *Robbins Report* (1965) and then the *Dearing Report* (1997) and the *Kennedy Report* (1997). We have considered the strategies employed to enable widening participation of under-represented groups by the various political parties, particularly the New Labour approach to widening participation and the evolving response of the Coalition government elected in 2010, and particularly the impact of the *Browne Report* (2010) in instrumentally driving the changing landscape of higher education provision.

From a lifelong learning perspective, higher education has played a significant part in enabling people to achieve their potential. Widening participation strategies have particularly enabled people to achieve a higher level of education using a variety of routes and pathways. This allows the individual and the state to continue being a success, both economically and socially.

Arguably, higher education is now positioned within a 'learning society' with a significant change of purpose that is required to be responsive to the pace of change – socially, economically and culturally.

5

Further education

This chapter will explore lifelong learning within the context of further education. Further education is likely to be the strand of lifelong learning you are most familiar with, but in this chapter I want you to consider the role and purpose of further education within a lifelong learning framework. We have discussed how adult and community learning works very successfully to support people who find themselves, for whatever reason, marginalised from mainstream society. Also, we have explored how lifelong learning has a key role to play in higher education, supporting a widening participation agenda. Both these strands very much work within a social justice framework, working with the ambition to ensure all members of our society have every opportunity to engage in learning and to achieve their potential.

I have drawn up three questions to enable your exploration of the further education strand of lifelong learning. Firstly, what does further education mean and represent? In this section we will consider the contribution of further education to lifelong learning. Secondly, what types of learners access further education provision? This is the biggest section of the chapter, and allows us to consider the role of further education in the contemporary UK. Particularly, we will consider the types of learning opportunities that are offered by further education providers, including adult language, literacy and numeracy programmes and vocational learning programmes, including the 14–19 Diploma group of qualifications.

The final question allows us to analyse the future of further education providers. What challenges do further education providers face? This question allows us to explore how further education providers are responding to the changes in our society: socially, economically and culturally. This is particularly important as we continue to be economically attractive to global markets and ensure our responsiveness to employers' demands for particular knowledge and skills. Additionally, we explore the funding mechanism that will support further education providers following the policy developments of the Coalition government.

What does further education mean and represent?

Further education is probably the most common area that people think about when considering lifelong learning. Further education is often the strand that sits outside the traditional academic route of primary, secondary and higher education, often being referred to as the 'Cinderella' strand of education, in that it sits outstand the perceived 'normal' progression. When you consider further education you may think of it as an area that caters particularly for students who elect to undertake vocational qualifications, rather than academic types of qualifications. We will explore the reality of this perspective in this chapter.

It is worth noting that the delivery of lifelong learning is messy. I have 'chunked' the provision of lifelong learning in an attempt to provide an overview of the broad and varied range of lifelong learning delivery and learning opportunities, but this is not as clean as you might have to come to presume in compulsory education – where education provision is mainly provided for a chronological age group and students broadly cover a similar curriculum, whether the education is delivered by the state or privately, with students working towards nationally recognised qualifications.

Further education colleges or providers most often offer learning opportunities for students of any age following completion of their compulsory education. For some students this is because their school does not offer post–GCSE learning opportunities, for others it is because their chosen programme of study is not provided by their school. However, further education is a much bigger and broader provider of lifelong learning opportunities for all members of our society, at any age, as will become apparent through this chapter.

Task

Before we review further education, take a few minutes to write down everything you know about it. Think about the following questions:

1. Why do people go to college?
2. What courses do further education colleges offer?
3. Who can access these courses?
4. Who pays for them?
5. How old are the students?
6. Do they study full time or part time?

Further education, as a strand of education, is often referred to as a 'Cinderella' addition to the framework of the traditional tertiary system. This has resulted in the strand struggling to develop a strong identity in terms of its role and purpose in delivering and providing learning opportunities. Historically, further education provision has most often been associated with vocational programmes. It has been regarded as providing learning opportunities for those who are not identified as capable of pursuing an academic programme of study, or provision that offers a 'second chance' to achieve qualifications traditionally expected to be achieved while in compulsory schooling. Alternatively, further education has long been associated with opportunities for adults to study part time in the evenings, either for socially focused benefits or to enable students to obtain qualifications that may be career related.

The importance of the further education sector has been recognised through a range of texts, but one of the most seminal reports that influenced the direction of further education provision was provided by Sir Andrew Foster who led an investigation in the future of further education colleges during 2004–2005. In his report (Foster, 2005) he identified a range of strengths within the further education sector, particularly the number of learners who accessed learning opportunities through college provision. He recognised and acknowledged the wide diversity of provision, evidencing a strong commitment to social inclusion by providers who offered programmes that were both flexible and adaptable. There was also evidence of college provision supporting local businesses by providing programmes that included the skills needed for those businesses. Foster also acknowledged the commitment of further education colleges to develop a professional and committed workforce. This was a very positive review of the further education strand of lifelong learning. However, Foster also identified key challenges: 'above all, FE lacks a clearly recognised and shared core purpose' (DfES, 2005: 6) and 'despite many good local examples, the relationships between employers and FE colleges is patchy and needs to be significantly improved. Employers have repeatedly said that FE colleges are not meeting their needs' (DfES, 2005: 43).

The *Foster Report* recognised that there was no single magical solution to the challenges faced by further education, and felt that a comprehensive set of reforms across the whole system should be undertaken to ensure that further education colleges could support economic achievement by helping individuals realise their personal potential – and hence provide the basis for a progressive enhancement in further education's standing in both the education community and society at large. In identifying these weaknesses, Foster provided a model for development which incorporated five imperatives, as outlined below. This cyclical model identifies areas that colleges needed to focus on and the strategic response they need to develop in order to position themselves competitively in an increasingly marketised sector of lifelong learning. In addressing these imperatives, Foster recommended that the further education sector needed to develop absolute clarity about their primary purpose: 'to improve employability and skills in its local area contributing to economic growth and social inclusion' (DfES, 2005: 10).

Five Imperatives of focus for further education (DfES, 2005):

- Purpose Imperative
- Quality Imperative
- Learners Imperative
- Employers Imperative
- Reputation Imperative

This renewed focus on employability skills led to charges by Bryan and Hayes (2007: 62) of 'the McDonaldalization of further education' with charges laid against further education that government messages were so confused that they did not know what it was that they should be producing, and that further education should be an area that focused on the development of skills, confidence, self-esteem and social inclusion rather than 'an education'.

Further education provision, over the last decade or so, has moved from one where there was a strong focus on vocational, remedial, second chance or part time learning for adults, either accredited for not, to one which has become a central and key provider of learning that is driven to meet the economic demands of the country. That said, contemporary further education college providers continue to offer a broad and varied range of learning opportunities, from initial or entry-level qualifications all the way through to higher education programmes. Further education colleges are often regarded as the first point of access for the majority of the population who have left compulsory education. According to the Association of Colleges in excess of three million people access learning opportunities through further education providers annually, engaging in academic programmes, apprenticeship programmes and a wide range of other programmes. One of the major areas of focus for colleges is to provide learning opportunities to people of all ages without discrimination.

What types of learners access further education provision?

If you have not explored the introductory chapters of this book, which explain some of the policies that have influenced the delivery of lifelong learning over the last decade, it is worth spending a few minutes reviewing how government policies have driven the curricula that are offered and how these have been particularly influenced by funding decisions. Below are some examples of the types of learning programmes that have been offered by further education colleges over the last two decades, which demonstrate how provision has evolved to reflect the focus of government thinking and decision making.

Over the last decade or so the change in terminology used to describe lifelong learning opportunities – from learning to education to training to skills – has informed the types of curricula that further education providers have delivered, and this has resulted in a constant requirement to refocus and change the priorities of lifelong learning programmes: from a focus on the development and delivery of adult literacy and numeracy programmes; to extending opportunities for the 14–19 age group; through the creation of 14–19 Diplomas; to a contemporary refocus on academic skills to ensure that young people in particular have the necessary skills to be able to traverse employment opportunities, but also to ensure they can exist effectively and independently in an increasingly knowledge-based society. Parallel to this, further education providers work closely with local employers to ensure that vocational programmes are 'fit for purpose' and have credibility and value for people seeking employment in a particular sector.

Adult literacy, language and numeracy programmes

At the start of the new millennium there was an increased focus by the then New Labour government on ensuring that the adult population had the necessary literacy and numeracy skills to be able to competently and effectively engage in economic activities, such as employment, and social activities, such as household finances. A key strategy developed to meet this ambition was the *Skills for Life* strategy (DfEE, 2001a). *Skills for Life: The National Strategy for Improving Adult Literacy and Numeracy Skills* was published in March 2001 with the aspiration: 'to give all adults in England the opportunity to acquire the skills for active participation in twenty-first-century society' (DfEE, 2001a: Foreword).

The rationale underpinning the strategy was to tackle and eradicate what had come to be perceived by policy-makers as the 'burden' of adults who were economically limited or inactive because their low levels of language, literacy and numeracy (LLN) prevented them from obtaining sustainable employment.

Reflection

Are you surprised that, in a developed country where we have had compulsory schooling for more than a century, at the beginning of the twenty-first century our government is producing a strategy aimed at eradicating low levels of literacy and numeracy in adults?

Is it unreasonable to presume that, given everyone has had to be exposed to 10–15 years of compulsory education, as a minimum everyone should complete their education with at least the skills of being able to read, write and undertake basic numeracy?

The strategy highlighted the groups that would become the priority focus of intervention, where needs were considered to be greatest and where it could potentially have the most influence. The strategy outlined how the government planned to tackle the issue of low LLN skills through the introduction of a suite of interventions, including:

Initiating radical changes to the education and training system for those learning literacy and numeracy skills in order to raise standards and boost levels of achievement. New national standards, new materials and a common core curriculum leading to national tests will make sure that the same approach to teaching and learning, based on the most effective practice, is adopted across the country. We [the government] are introducing new, more effective ways of assessing need and better teacher training and setting up a new research centre and rigorous national inspections to monitor standards.

(DfEE, 2001a: 7)

The national curricula for adult literacy and numeracy were constructed to provide a framework in which *Skills for Life* teaching and learning could take place. The curricula provided teachers with a comprehensive framework to help identify and meet learners' individual learning needs. For teachers and learners alike, the introduction of core curricula ensured a common approach to LLN teaching and course content. To further support the development of LLN skills, national tests for adult literacy and numeracy were also developed and launched in September 2001.

A central aim of the strategy was to raise teaching standards among adult literacy and numeracy teachers who previously had little scope or opportunity to acquire accredited qualifications in the teaching of their subject. Since September 2002 a new professional programme has been put in place to enable teachers specialising in teaching adult literacy and numeracy to meet the requirements of the national standards by undertaking a subject specialist qualification.

Since its launch, the *Skills for Life* strategy (DfEE, 2001a) has become the biggest overarching policy drive that has ever taken place in post-compulsory education in England. It was supported by significant investment from government (Crawley, 2005) and has changed the landscape in which LLN is conceptually understood and provided. There is evidence of LLN teaching and learning across all strands of lifelong learning, with further education providers leading the way in developing and delivering a broad range of LLN programmes.

While the *Skills for Life* strategy gave adult literacy and numeracy teaching and learning a priority focus during the first decade of the twenty-first century, it was not without its critics, from learners, teachers and employers alike. Teachers complained that they were not being given enough time within the funding demands of programmes to be able to support learners effectively in developing their skills. Also, they complained that some programmes were only focusing on the skills that would enable them to pass the tests that learners were required to complete at the end of their programme. Learners similarly complained that the tests were not meeting their needs in terms of the skills they needed in order to mediate their life effectively. Additionally, learners complained that they felt uncomfortable undertaking a literacy or numeracy course as it was built on a model of 'what you can't do', which felt very negative, and instead suggested they would rather undertake English and mathematics programmes which were more commonly understood by the population. Employers also complained that they did not understand the new qualifications for literacy and numeracy, being unclear about the levels of the qualifications and the terminology that was incorporated into literacy and numeracy. As well as placing little value on the qualification, employers stated that even with these qualifications people were often still unable to complete simple literacy and numeracy tasks.

Functional Skills

In response to these challenges, government worked to introduce a new suite of qualifications called Functional Skills. Functional Skills are a set of qualifications covering English, mathematics and information and communication technology (ICT) (note the return to the familiar terminology, and the introduction of a technology qualification). They were developed as a response to the demands of employers, who identified these particular skills gaps when trying to recruit staff, and were planned for national implementation in September 2010. It was expected that this suite of qualifications would replace *Skills for Life* qualifications. Unique to these qualifications was a new approach to accreditation, in that tests would adopt a flexible assessment structure that could be adapted to the needs of individual learners, and that tests would reflect real-life settings enabling learners to apply newly developed literacy and numeracy skills to everyday requirements.

The new Functional Skills qualifications have taken longer than expected to be embedded into lifelong learning provision, partly as a result to the change in government and a refocusing of other qualifications, such as Diplomas (discussed below), which when developed were closely linked to Functional Skills qualifications. However, they are becoming the preferred model for the delivery of adult literacy and numeracy qualifications, seeing the phasing out of *Skills for Life* qualifications.

Vocational programmes and 14–19 Diplomas

The delivery of vocationally focused learning programmes has been the traditional specialism of the further education strand of lifelong learning. Many young people and adults wishing to train or learn new skills turn to their local college to seek learning programmes that enable them to achieve vocationally relevant qualifications. These programmes can range from secretarial, hairdressing, catering and construction programmes, conventionally considered to result in semi-skilled employment, to higher-level training, including accounting or engineering, leading to more skilled employment opportunities. Such programmes have come to be delivered through a range of models, including full time or part time in college, as 'blended' programmes with learners attending both work placements and college for different parts of their study, to ones that are wholly situated within the work environment.

During the last decade (2000–2010) there was an increasing recognition that some learners were more engaged in learning programmes that appeared to be more meaningful for them because they had a particular interest in a specific area of employment. In an ambitious programme to bring together meaningful learning in the form of a vocational element, the need to ensure that learners continued to develop literacy and numeracy capability, and also to ensure programmes were 'fit for purpose' in terms of the area of employment focus, the government worked with stakeholders to develop 14–19 Diplomas.

These were groundbreaking for a number of reasons. Firstly, perhaps arguably for the first time, they broke the traditional boundary of compulsory education, with compulsory education appearing to end at the age of 16, and post-compulsory education commencing at 16. Also, they required partners to come together to work to develop vocationally relevant programmes with traditional academic skills, meaning that schools, colleges and employers needed to come together to develop meaningful qualifications.

The 14–19 Diplomas refer to a suite of qualifications that were developed and first introduced in 2008 to respond to a range of challenges and charges directed towards school and college provision. Vocational qualifications, delivered through further education providers have, as we have seen, often been regarded as second-class qualifications, with academic qualifications routinely being given higher esteem. The development of 14–19 Diplomas were introduced to respond to this challenge, by introducing a strong theoretical rigour to the study of vocational qualifications.

The Diploma delivery model required partnership collaboration and input from schools, colleges and employers. It was expected that such collaboration would enable young people to be motivated and engaged in their learning programme, as it was applied to a particular area of employment, and achieve a robust and employment-relevant qualification. The Diploma was regarded by many to be the qualification that was going to bridge, and ultimately abolish, the academic–vocational divide.

The qualification was established as a national entitlement to all young people between the ages of 14 and 19, resulting in schools, employers and further education and other training providers being compelled to collaborate in the development of the programmes. Throughout the planning, development and delivery of Diplomas, 17 subject areas were identified covering a range of occupational sectors of the economy, and to be phased in over a four-year period with all 17 being available by

2013. By 2008 the first four Diplomas were ready for delivery – ICT, health and social care, engineering, and creative and media.

Diplomas could be studied at three levels: Foundation (Level 1), Higher (Level 2) and Advanced (Level 3), with the first two being available to learners from the age of 14. The Diplomas had three components: a generic element common to all those studying them, which included the functional skills element discussed above and a minimum of ten days' work experience; some principal learning which focused on the area of vocational relevance; and some additional learning which could include GCSEs or A levels depending on the level of Diploma you were studying. The Diplomas were assessed through a mixture of exams and coursework.

However, the Diploma qualification faced many challenges, not least the capacity of providers to work in partnership to provide the qualification. By the arrival of the Coalition government, flaws in the qualifications were starting to be identified and the roll out of the Diplomas was halted by Michael Gove, the new education minister. Initially Diplomas were reoffered not as an entitlement for all young people, but rather as an optional choice. Schools and colleges would be allowed to choose how many and which, if any, Diploma subjects they offered their students. The development of the remaining Diplomas was cancelled.

It was argued that he demise of the Diploma was largely because employers did not understand the qualification, which is surprising as a mandatory requirement for the planning, development and delivery of Diplomas was the involvement of employers. It is impossible to state whether such a programme would have been successful in achieving equality between vocational and academic programmes as the programme did not run for long enough to be evaluated.

The *Wolf Report* (2011)

Following the relaxation of mandatory requirements to offer Diplomas collaboratively through consortia, Gove asked Professor Alison Wolf to undertake a review of the current range of vocational qualifications, to enable him to make an informed decision about the value of the qualification for contemporary UK society going forward. The remit of the review given to Wolf was to look at the organisation of vocational education and consider its responsiveness to a changing labour market, and also to consider ways to increase incentives for young people to participate in vocational learning programmes. The review was also asked to highlight good practice where it was found. In developing the remit for the review it was expected that Wolf and her colleagues would also examine the institutional arrangements for vocational education, funding mechanisms associated with such provision, progression opportunities from vocational education into higher education and higher-level training and, interestingly, the role of other providers of vocational education, particularly the third sector, private training providers and employers.

Wolf reported her findings in March 2011, making 27 recommendations for the overhaul and reform of vocational education. Wolf found that the current system was complex, costly and often counterproductive, suggesting that some learners were being guided to undertake vocational courses that she described as 'inferior', and which had little or no value in the employment market. However, she also identified many vocational qualifications that were excellent.

The *Wolf Report* (Wolf, 2011) concluded that the framework of vocational qualifications required reform in order to ensure that all those participating in such programmes were given a fair chance of receiving a good education, and also be well positioned to obtain a good job. As part of this reform, she identified that all vocational programmes for the future should require all participants to achieve at least a grade 'C' in English and mathematics. In contradiction of the previously developed Diplomas, Wolf argued that young people aged 14–16 should continue to spend the majority of the time focusing their studies on a shared academic core of subjects, rather than any study that might be regarded as vocational.

Some in the sector felt the report to be a damming indictment of the hard work that had been undertaken previously to develop vocationally relevant qualifications. However, when Gove received Wolf's report he commented that it was both 'brilliant and ground-breaking' (DfE, online). The adoption of some the report's recommendations were regarded as having potentially far-reaching implications for all sectors of education and strands of lifelong learning, particularly in enabling teachers to teach across the education sectors, a transmobility which up until this point had been fiercely opposed by the compulsory sector of education (a discussion regarding the workforce for the lifelong learning sector can be located in Chapter 2).

In describing the current vocational education system, Wolf identified five key labour market characteristics that vocational programmes should be able to respond to. These were:

1. A shift towards full-time participation up to the age of 19 (this refers to the move of compulsory education to require all young people to continue their involvement in education until a minimum age of 18 by 2015);

2. A reduction in employment opportunities for 16–17 year olds (this recognises that there are less and less opportunities for those leaving compulsory education at 16 with Level 2 qualifications to achieve and sustain employment);

3. A growing emphasis on the importance of work experience (this characteristic recognises the demand of contemporary employers who want to see evidence of both academic capability and work experience, which can take many forms including volunteering, paid part-time work or internships);

4. A consistently high premium on having English and mathematics qualifications (this characteristic reflects both the Coalition's ambition and employers' demands that these skills are required in order for individuals to be successful in employment and in society more generally); and

5. A recognition of job mobility and flexibility (this characteristic reflects an acknowledgment that people are more likely to be engaged in a range of employment during their lifetimes in light of advances in technology, and as such vocational programmes should incorporate skills that are transferable between employers and employment opportunities).

Throughout this report, colleges were granted the pivotal role of ensuring the reforms of vocational qualifications were undertaken and were 'fit for purpose'.

> ## Task
>
> Download the *Wolf Report* and analyse the recommendations: https://www.education.gov.uk/publications/eOrderingDownload/The%20Wolf%20Report.pdf
>
> And then have a look at the government response to the report: https://www.education.gov.uk/publications/eOrderingDownload/Wolf-Review_Response.pdf
>
> Consider the following questions:
>
> ■ Do you think that the recommendations are useful?
> ■ Will the government be able to implement the recommendations?
> ■ Do you think learners will benefit from new vocational qualifications?
> ■ How can we ensure that employers will understand the new qualifications?
> ■ What other issues can you identify?
>
> And then consider the following questions:
>
> ■ Do you think that such an approach to qualification development, including lifelong learning providers and employers, is useful?
> ■ How might such an approach compromise the range of learning programmes made available to society?

What challenges do further education providers face?

The role of further education college provision has evolved with the election of the new Coalition government, and the development of new delivery strategies that frame the future of further education going forward.

The two key documents that have, and will continue to, inform the role, purpose and mission of further education college provision are the *Skills for Sustainable Growth* strategy published by the Department for Business Innovations and Skills (DBIS) in November 2010, and subsequently the paper entitled *New Challenges, New Chances: Further Education and Skills System Reform Plan: Building a World Class Skills System* in December 2011. The key features of each of these publications are outlined below.

Skills for Sustainable Growth (DBIS, 2010b)

This document, as outlined in earlier chapters, forms the framework through which the whole lifelong learning system in contemporary UK society will be facilitated, resourced and focused under the guidance of the Coalition government. Using their three guiding principles of 'fairness, freedom and responsibility', the government outlines an agenda for change.

In publishing this strategy document, the government positions lifelong learning as a key instrument that can contribute to the country's ability to achieve sustainable economic growth and extend social inclusion and upward social mobility. It is hoped that this will be accomplished by improving the population's skills, resulting in the creation of a world-class skills base that provides the UK with a competitive advantage in global markets.

The strategy puts a high-quality further education sector at the heart of its ambitions for reform.

New Challenges, New Chances (DBIS, 2011b)

Following on from the *Skills for Sustainable Growth* strategy, and focusing specifically on the further education strand of lifelong learning, in December 2011 the Coalition published *New Challenges, New Chances: Further Education and Skills System Reform Plan: Building a World Class Skills System*. This reform plan sets out the key elements of the reform programme for the system as outlined below:

- Students put at the heart of the further education and skills system, by ensuring opportunities for informed choices are available;
- First-class advice delivered by the National Careers Service, by providing learners with the information they need to capitalise on their learning opportunities;
- A ladder of opportunity of comprehensive vocational education and training programmes provided by programmes giving opportunities for progression beyond further education into higher vocational education;
- Excellence in teaching and learning encouraged by reviewing professionalism in the FE and skills workforce;
- Relevant and focused learning programmes and qualifications developed by taking action to ensure that qualifications are of high quality and are easy to understanding through consultations with employers;
- Strategic governance created for a dynamic further education sector, by enabling colleges to take the lead in developing delivery models to meet the needs of their communities;
- Freedoms and flexibilities increased by reducing bureaucracy in the system;
- Funding priorities streamlined through a simplified funding system, by ensuring that funding focuses on high-quality provision that delivers good value for money and is both innovative and responsive to local circumstances;
- Students empowered so they make informed choices, by providing quality information that is accessible; and
- The globalisation of further education encouraged, by supporting the sector to take advantage of opportunities in the global market.

By focussing the system in this way it is expected to 'fuel individual achievement, power the common good and drive upward economic performance' (DBIS, 2011b: 3).

This is a comprehensive, and some might say a somewhat daunting, list of expectations for the further education sector. It highlights some important changes for the landscape of further education, provides opportunities to broaden and extend provision, but for some might also appear limited. There is much said about vocational provision and learning for economic outcome, leading to increased prosperity for the country, but little evidence of support for learning opportunities that may not directly lead to increased opportunities for employment, or learning for social engagement that may be informal and non-credit bearing. These are challenges for further education colleges as they enter the next stage of change.

Task

Download the executive summary of these documents (they are both available on the Department for Business, Innovation and Skills website) and familiarise yourself with the key arguments and ambitions that the government has set out for the further education sector.

- Do you think these ambitions are reasonable?
- Are they achievable?
- Do you think that this is the correct focus for our contemporary UK society?
- Could you offer an alternative model?

A word about funding

During the first decade of the millennium, and in line with the then government's widening participation strategy (see Chapter 4 on higher education for a detailed discussion of this strategy), students were encouraged to continue to engage with their studies following completion of their Level 2 qualifications, and to engage in Level 3 qualifications that would enable them to apply for and secure a place in higher education or obtain higher-skilled employment.

One of the major intervention and support strategies that were created to assist students in this endeavour was the development of the Education Maintenance Allowance (EMA). This means-tested grant was offered to students whose household income fell below a certain level. There were three levels of EMA, with students receiving either £10, £20 or £30 per week to support them with their travel costs and living costs while attending college. However, there were requirements imposed on students who were in receipt of this benefit. Students were required to provide evidence of attendance at their learning programme by registering at each class – should they fail to attend any of their lectures, punitive measures would result in terms of withdrawal of EMA.

Such intervention did lead to an increase in attendance at further education provision by students who may not otherwise have been able to afford to go to college, but there has been a range of questions and challenges to this intervention, not least the need to declare your parents' income, resulting in some students not accessing the financial support. Other concerns raised included: the underlying reasons and motivations of students to attend training programmes; the usefulness of the training programme in terms of its value to possible future employers; and the perceived inequality between students who needed to undertake part-time work to support themselves and those in receipt of EMA who did not.

The election of the Coalition government has seen a refocus of funding for students undertaking any lifelong learning opportunity, including an ambition to introduction lifelong learning accounts (LLA) and the introduction of further education loans for students over the age of 24 undertaking learning programmes at Level 3 or above (re-read the *Skills for Sustainable Growth* strategy above for more details on the changing funding models for the further education system).

One of the key changes made by the Coalition government in relation to funding was the replacement of the EMA allowance with a new, smaller, discretionary grant. This grant will be administered by local providers to those students considered to be most in need of financial assistance. The scheme is made up of two parts: (1) students who are identified as most vulnerable will be eligible for bursaries of £1,200 per academic year; and (2) schools and colleges will then be able to, with discretion, award bursaries to students who may be facing genuine financial barriers to participating in their learning programmes, such as the cost of transport, food or equipment. This second payment can be given in varying amounts and could be paid weekly, monthly or annually. Schools will also be able to link other requirements to the bursary payment, such as minimum levels of attendance or certain behaviours.

Once again a series of challenges arise, including the reduction in funding resulting in fewer people being able to access the fund. Also, as the fund is administered locally providers are able to interpret the regulations which may result in students receiving varying amounts of support, depending on their location or the college provider themselves.

Reflection

1. List the reasons why you think a government might want to support young people to continue in educational provision.

2. Think about the economic needs of the country – the skills demanded by employers and also the cost to the country of having young people who are not in education and unable to secure and maintain employment. Do you think the government is ambitious in its support of young people to achieve social mobility by providing them with as much support as possible to access and gain the highest possible qualifications that will, in turn, enable them to secure professional employment opportunities?

The future for further education colleges

In thinking about the role and identity of further education colleges for the future, Howard (2009: 11–13) puts forward a framework that colleges should consider and refer to as they prepare for their future, as shown below:

1. Colleges should form the 'institutional backbone' of the lifelong learning system, with a renewed remit for adult learning;

2. Colleges' values and missions should be inclusive and pluralistic, offering a comprehensive and diverse curriculum for a diverse adult population;

3. Colleges should be first and foremost local organisations, playing a leading role in a coherent networked system with a single point of entry for learners;

4. Colleges should take the lead in rethinking, developing and modelling adult pedagogies and models of learning provision which are enhanced by new technologies and suit the future patterns of adults' lives, work and social commitments in the twenty-first century;

5. Colleges should offer a core citizens curriculum; and

6. Vocational education, including work-based training and professional development from Level 1 to postgraduate, should remain central to colleges' missions.

Task

Ensure you are familiar with any new terminology in this framework, for example 'pluralistic' and 'pedagogy'. Consider the following questions:

1. What do you think Howard means by a citizen curriculum? What should it contain? Who would study it? How? Why?
2. Should colleges focus only on adults? Is this different from the 16–19 age group?
3. What do you think further education colleges should prioritise?

Summary

This chapter has set out the role of further education colleges as part of the lifelong learning sector. It has tracked the evolution of the role and purpose of further education colleges through a New Labour government, through to a Coalition government. Along the way, we have considered the types of learning opportunities that have been provided by further education colleges, particularly adult literacy, language and numeracy programmes, and vocational programmes, examining how government policy has driven and changed the curriculum provided by further education colleges. We then went on to consider how further education colleges are positioning themselves for the future, and how they are responding to the challenges and changes in contemporary UK society, not least the current economic climate.

You have been invited, throughout the chapter, to think critically about the evolving nature of further education colleges and their responses to the demands made upon them by our government. The challenge that is clearly evident for the further education strand of the lifelong learning sector is that it is required to be all things for all people: to take responsibility for ensuring that local employers have the necessary skills base among potential employees to ensure recruitment to vacancies can be readily achieved; to provide social learning for an aging population; to ensure the equality of the programmes offered regardless of the demographic or ethnic mix of the community; to provide academic qualifications for those who wish to pursue such qualifications and vocational qualifications for those who are pursuing an alternative pathway; and to provide basic skills for those who have been unable to develop those skills.

At the same time, funding for further education is driven by government agendas and that necessarily influences a changing curriculum focus based on policy decisions. Funding has been relocated to one post-16 agency – the Skills Funding Agency – and as a government quango (quasi-autonomous non-governmental organisation) it is directed to fund particular curriculum areas that inform the construction of an economically active and socially just society (arguable very good moral values). However, it is particularly challenging when funding is limited to a particular focus, with participants increasingly expected to contribute to learning programmes which are seen to hold economic merit.

If further education is being tasked by government policy to save our economy, by ensuring that citizens all have the necessary skills to be able to contribute to the economic prosperity of the country, then does that compromise the social purpose of learning and vice versa?

Reflection

Armed with your developing awareness of learning opportunities provided by further education colleges, go online and have a look at a few college prospectus to see what other types of learning programmes are being delivered. Ask yourself whether all the programmes:

- Have a qualification outcome;
- Are part time or full time;
- Are academic or vocational;
- Are offered at a range of levels;
- Can be identified as having a specific link to employment opportunities;
- Appear to be for social interest; and
- Are focussed to a particular age group.

6

Work-based learning

In the previous chapter we explored further education, and I suggested that most people think about lifelong learning as happening in a local further education college. When people think about why people might engage in lifelong learning it is common to think that learning after compulsory education takes place within the context of employment – either to progress in current employment, or to be able to change career paths. This chapter will explore lifelong learning that can be considered to be 'work-based'.

Firstly, this chapter will look at lifelong learning and pre-employment, exploring learning opportunities for unemployed adults that enable them to develop employability skills. This section will consider what is meant by 'employability', and introduce the Work Programme, a government initiative aimed at working with unemployed individuals to develop the necessary skills to enable them to obtain and sustain employment.

The chapter will then consider who the key providers and supporters of lifelong learning in a work-based lifelong learning environment are, particularly employment and learning providers, Unionlearn and sector skills councils (SSCs). This part will then go on to consider the choices adults have to engage in work-based learning programmes.

Lastly, we will consider the key framework through which work-based learning is being developed in response to employer demand through contemporary UK government policy: the apprenticeship framework.

Introduction

Work-based learning is a long-term and well-established model of focused learning in work, while being simultaneously presented as a relatively new phenomenon where people can learn together in a familiar environment but engage in learning which is not focused on either their current employment needs or potential future employment opportunities.

While this chapter explores lifelong learning and work-based learning, prior this it is important to establish the meaning of some key terminology, particularly employability.

Lifelong learning and pre-employment programmes

Employability

While employment can readily be defined as a contract between two parties – the employer and the employee – and unemployment can be seen as the condition of not having employment, employability sits at the interface of these two concepts and informs many of the initiatives developed, particularly by government, to enable people to move from a state of unemployment to one of employment. Employability is described by Finn (2000: 387) as 'the key to future social cohesion and job security'.

Employability, notably, refers to a person's capability of gaining initial employment, maintaining employment and consequently obtaining new employment if necessary. Importantly, employability indicates an individual's capability to move self-sufficiently and independently within the labour market. Such employability is reliant on the specific knowledge, skills and attitudes that an individual possesses, the way these can be used in future employment and how these are presented to prospective employers.

While employability skills have traditionally been closely associated with vocational and academic skills, there is a series of wider associated skills required by employers to ensure successful entry into the labour market, such as information about the labour market and appropriate training pathways, where necessary, to support entry into different sectors of employment.

Commonly, discussions regarding employability, and the ability of an individual to become employed and sustain employment, are articulated through three main elements (Hillage and Pollard in Finn, 2000: 387):

1. The ability to gain initial employment, hence the interest in ensuring that 'key skills', careers advice and an understanding of the world of work are embedded in the education system;

2. The ability to maintain employment and make 'transitions' between jobs and roles within the same organisation to meet new job requirements; and

3. The ability to obtain new employment if required, that is, to be independent in the labour market by being willing and able to manage employment transitions between and within organisations.

Improving employability was at the centre of the New Labour government's employment strategy. Employability skills were identified as the key to modernising the country, ensuring it was economically competitive and continued to be socially cohesive. Their aim was to 'build security through employability' by helping people to develop and adapt their skills as the needs of the labour market and economy changed (DfEE in Finn, 2000: 384).

Ongoing government welfare to work policies have been aimed at developing training programmes that can accredit employability skills by providing frameworks through which individuals can be supported to move from unemployment to employment, drawing on three key elements: (1) raising basic standards of education; (2) the creation of a culture of lifelong learning; and (3) the use of the welfare to work strategy.

Task

Try and list as many skills as possible, that you would consider to be employability skills. I will start you off:

- Time management
- Organisation Skills
- Confidence

Welfare to work programmes

Welfare to work programmes have been part of the UK's welfare system for more than a century, since the introduction of the first *National Insurance Act* in 1911. This Act aimed to provide a comprehensive programme of financial assistance to those people who found themselves unemployed. Prior to this Act unemployed workers historically sought support through the Poor Law system (Wu, 2000). The *National Insurance Act* (Great Britain, 1911) provides the foreground for today's welfare system, and it is noteworthy that what was the focus for inclusion in the system in the early 1900s continues today. A major reform and overhaul of the system was undertaken in 1994 when the then Conservative government introduced a new type of unemployment benefit: Jobseeker's Allowance.

Upon election in 1997, the New Labour government linked welfare assistance with employment and the requirements of the country for future economic success. The government at the time aimed to invest:

> heavily in education and training, aiming to improve productivity through tackling a range of skills shortages, along with introducing a crusade to improve adult basic skills in literacy and numeracy.
>
> (DWP, 2001: 25)

Welfare to work programmes formed part of the New Labour government's strategy to diminish the problem of long-term unemployment (DfEE, 2001a; Webb, 2003), incorporating three main elements: welfare to work policies; targeted measures to help areas of the country and groups of people facing the most significant barriers to work; and policies to strengthen work incentives (Webb, 2003). 'Jobcentre Plus' became the name for the Working Age Agency responsible for the delivery of these policies. Its objective was to deliver work-focused support for all those of working age on out-of-work benefits – both unemployed and economically inactive. A series of intervention education and training programmes were developed and introduced to assist long-term unemployed adults develop the skills needed to re-enter the labour market, under the umbrella of Work-Based Learning for Adults, and included programmes such as basic employability programmes, which included a focus on the development of adult literacy and numeracy skills, employability skills and occupational skills.

The Work Programme

Since the election of the Coalition government, the welfare system in the UK has been reviewed and developed. The government continues to recognise the importance of employability skills and has developed a new overarching welfare programme as part of a welfare reform programme that replaces the suite of umbrella programmes provided prior to its election, called the Work Programme.

The Work Programme was introduced in June 2011 (DWP, 2011). The programme has been developed with the ambition of providing tailored and individual support for unemployed adults to enable them to effectively seek employment, and overcome any barriers that may be preventing them from both finding and sustaining employment. The programme is seem as a partnership between government and Work Programme providers who are drawn from across the public, private and third sectors. This programme replaces all pre-existing welfare programmes.

The feature that distinguishes it from its predecessors is that providers of the programme are paid 'on results'. This means that providers are incentivised to achieve the outcome for the programme – to assist individuals in achieving sustainable employment – through whatever interventions are necessary, whether that is additional training or work experience.

The pros and cons of lifelong learning for the unemployed

Prior to the introduction of the Work Programme, unemployed adults were required to attend training programmes to increase their employability skills, which were identified as: literacy and numeracy skills; work experience; and softer skills including how to apply for a job, developing an effective curriculum vitae and undertaking a successful interview, all aimed at increasing an individual's confidence and capability to undertake employment. However, adults who attended such programmes often felt compromised as they were only able to access such training programmes for limited periods of time – up to 26 weeks – and often were unable to access them until they had been unemployed for 12 months, with adults often leaving halfway through a learning programme and regularly unable to complete a qualification. Such challenges have been eradicated with the introduction of the new Work Programme. Under the new programme, unemployed adults are eligible for entry to the programme almost immediately, working with a specialist to assist them in developing the necessary skills that will enable them to re-enter to local labour market. The new programme is seen as a much more 'fit for purpose' programme.

However, those in receipt of welfare reform are 'conditioned' or obliged to undertake certain activities, and are served with sanctions should they decide not to engage in the activities asked of them. If an unemployed adult is invited to undertake the Work Programme and declines, they may receive sanctions against them in the form of benefit withdrawal.

The Work Programme is a radical new programme and it will be worth watching to see how lifelong learning as part of the programme can assist adults in achieving employment.

Reflection

You can see from the above discussion how engagement in lifelong learning can have an extremely economic focus, due to having targeted employment outcomes. Consider the following questions:

- Should the unemployed be obliged to undertake programmes, including learning, to enhance their employability skills?
- Should adults be able to choose not to attend such programmes, and seek employment independently?
- Should adults be expected to undertake either lifelong learning programmes and/or work experience as part of the conditions of receiving welfare benefits?
- Should adults be disqualified from receiving welfare benefits if they choose not to engage in welfare programmes?

Who provides lifelong learning programmes in a work-based environment?

There are various groups, organisations and institutions who work to support lifelong learning opportunities in the workplace. As I have suggested, all strands of the lifelong learning sector can often be found working across learning environments, and this strand of lifelong learning is no different. It is not uncommon, for example, for further education providers, third sector providers, higher education providers and private training providers all to be providing learning opportunities onsite in an employer's organisation, as well as the employer themselves providing lifelong learning opportunities. Some of the key stakeholders who support and provide work-based learning are outlined below.

Continuing professional development

Work-based learning opportunities have traditionally been identified as continuing professional development (CPD). Employers can offer their employees a range of work-related training opportunities, which can include, for example, management training programmes, accountancy training or computer programme training. Such programmes can be delivered 'in-house' by existing staff, often drawn from human resource departments in larger organisations, and are not necessary associated with a qualification outcome. Participants often do receive a certificate from the employer to confirm their attendance on the programme, but this certificate has limited 'currency' in that it is often not recognised by other employers in the same way as more national qualifications such as GCSEs, A Levels or degree qualifications.

However, continuing professional development also exists for those who are qualified in a particular profession who are required to engage in, and undertake, targeted learning programmes to ensure their knowledge remains contemporary, current and useful. Examples of such professions include law and medicine. Such professions are often governed by associations that are membership organisations, and people wishing to practice their particular profession are required to become a member.

Task

Can you think of other professions that are required to undertake mandatory training to maintain their professional status?

Perhaps the obvious profession that I have not mentioned is the teaching profession. All teachers are required, following completion of their initial teacher training, to become a member of their governing membership organisation. Teachers practicing in the compulsory sector of education are required to undertake at least five days per year of continuing professional training, often termed 'inset' days.

Task

What continuing professional development activities are required for those practicing in the lifelong learning sector?

Start by exploring the role of the Institute for Learning website: www.ifl.ac.uk

---

Unionlearn

Unionlearn is the learning and skills organisation, or branch, of the Trade Union Congress (TUC) (an umbrella organisation working with trade unions across a range of employment areas to campaign for fair and equal treatment of employees). The key focus of Unionlearn is to work with trade unions to enable them to develop, plan and deliver learning opportunities for their members. The framework they use to support their work operates through union learning representatives (ULRs). These people are identified by their individual unions, and with the support of their employers, and are trained to signpost employees to lifelong learning opportunities. These training programmes are sometimes made available on-site within the work environment, or provided locally by a range of training providers.

Unionlearn have been instrumental over the last decade in promoting and supporting lifelong learning opportunities within employer environments. They have not only worked with unions to demonstrate the economic value to employers of engaging in learning opportunities but also the social benefits of engaging in learning opportunities which are not directly related to their area of employment.

Adult and employment learning providers

Private learning providers, or independent providers, are organisations that deliver lifelong learning programmes for profit. Much of the work of such organisations is contracted by employers or other funders, particularly government, to deliver specific programmes and packages of lifelong learning, for example the Work Programme discussed above. Private learning providers, along with other lifelong learning sector organisations, can belong to the Association of Employment and Learning Providers (AELP), a national membership organisation that supports providers who engage in government-funded skills training and employability programmes. Many of these organisations are contracted to deliver adult vocational lifelong learning skills provision, particularly in the form of apprenticeship training (discussed below). In addition, the AELP work with policy-makers to add their voice in the development of effective policy in this area.

Sector Skills Councils

Sector Skills Councils are a network of organisations, licensed by government, to provide employer leadership support and facilitate them in developing the necessary skills within their sector of employment to ensure they can continue to compete in an increasingly competitive economic market. They aim to encourage employers to invest in skills training in order to make possible and increase enterprise and create employment opportunities. Sector Skills Councils were brought under an alliance, or group, in 2008 to support their work. Some of the key priority areas of work that Sector Skills Councils are involved with include the establishment of sector standards and qualifications that are appropriate to employers.

It is evident that the above organisations are all involved in supporting lifelong learning in workplace environments. It is interesting to note that such learning programmes can cover all levels of learning and a very broad curriculum. What unites them is their general tendency to focus on learning programmes that can enhance employer capability or productivity, often resulting in the potential for increased economic activity and success. Some of these programmes are linked to accredited qualifications, but many are not.

One of the significant challenges for work-based learning providers is the engagement of participants. This may seem a contradictory observation, as there is often a clear relationship between employment and the learning programmes. However, the motivation to engage in mandatory training is often limited as a result of lack of choice to engage.

Reflection

Take a couple of minutes to think about some of the learning programmes you have been engaged in to date.

- You may have been asked to participate in some computer training as part of a part time job you are undertaking to earn some extra funds.
- You may have been asked to undertake some health and safety training in relation to some volunteering you have been undertaking.
- You may have been told that you can no longer engage in working with a particular group – for example occasional tennis coaching, guitar lessons or horse-riding lessons – unless you undertake training to obtain the necessary qualifications.

Would you approach the training programme differently if you:

(a) Chose to undertake the training?
(b) Were told you had to undertake the programme?

Do you think that individuals engage with lifelong learning programmes in different ways?

Choice to engage in work-based learning

Choice is a word often used and understood in our contemporary society. Simplistically, it suggests the selection of an item out of a number of options. In reality, for those engaged in work-based lifelong learning provision, however, there are often very few, if any, options available. Earlier in this chapter I described how those who are in receipt of welfare benefits are required to engage in activity, which can include lifelong learning, as part of the 'conditions' of receiving their benefits. In this section I examine some of the literature that considers choice, and explore whether lifelong learning programmes have been assembled in such a way that they detrimentally influence both choice and decision making for adults. Implicit in this discussion is the perception that adults are in a position where they have the 'freedom' to choose.

While it must be acknowledged that there is a wide range of literature on the subject of 'choice' that can be drawn from a range of disciplines, including economics, politics, law, philosophy and psychology, this literature review will necessarily focus on literature relating to opportunities of educational choice and models of economic choice associated with educational frameworks. However, it is important to recognise that much of the literature associated with notions of choice is framed within the 'compulsory' years of schooling for all stakeholders involved – there is little direct literature relating to adult choice within the post-16 sector of education and training.

'Choice' is described by Foskett and Hemsley-Brown (2001) as a social and political battleground wherein tensions exist between the rights of individuals to make choices and define their own existence, and the rights and obligations of the communities and societies within which they live (Foskett and Hemsley-Brown, 2001). It is not unreasonable to conclude that, as individuals, we are the products of the choices we make. However, many choices and decisions that inform our lives are not always under our control.

As we have discussed elsewhere is this book, within the contemporary UK the education system comprises a period of compulsory education from approximately 'rising' 5 to aged 16, and education undertaken following this age is referred to a post-compulsory education. In reality, however, there are so few choices available to young people at the age of 16 that, in reality, their choices are largely limited to different education and training pathways, such as vocational, apprenticeship or academic. Even though 'compulsion' is said not to exist within the post-compulsory sector – the lifelong learning sector – examples of recent government policies can be found which draw on economic and social expectations to ensure engagement in training programmes.

Theories of choice are predominantly constructed from models of economics (Foskett and Hemsley-Brown, 2001). Choice is identified as a central process for an individual, requiring him or her to engage in a decision-making processes that involves: (1) the construction and consideration of a range of options; and then subsequently (2) choosing between them. Such decision-making processes can be described as 'dynamic and incremental' in character, with choice preferences changing over time in response to external factors, such as media advertising and changing circumstances. Such a view of choice and decision making is based on four key elements (Foskett and Hemsley-Brown, 2001: 29):

1. That individuals will seek to maximise the benefits they will gain from the choices they make – so-called, utility maximisation;

2. That individuals will make choices that are entirely based on self-interest;

3. That choices will be made after a process of vigilant information collection; and

4. That the process of considering alternatives and making choices will be entirely rational.

Task

Take a minute to think about these four elements of choice and decision making. Do you recognise them?

Do you think all adults have the capacity and capability to make informed decisions and choices? If not, how can we ensure that all members of society have equal opportunities to make choices that are in their best interests?

The model of choice and decision making presented by Foskett and Hemsley-Brown (2001) is a very dynamic one in which individuals are perceived to hold all the knowledge and skills necessary to make considered choices. For many adult learners, however, such a dynamic approach to choice and decision making is unrealistic and unreasonable. Many require support and detailed information, advice and guidance to navigate the range of materials to enable them to make informed decisions and subsequent choices.

Often, there is no decision to be made about whether to participate in a training programme, or choice about which training programme might be most effective or appropriate, because a problem has not been self-identified. The ability to choose a training programme is not only closely associated with an individual's capacity for decision making but their motivation, or desire, to undertake such a programme.

Motivation to engage in work-based lifelong learning

Motivation is a term often associated with desire – a desire to learn, to engage, to participate, to commit, to progress and is defined by Curzon as 'a person's aroused desire for participation in a learning process' (Curzon, 1990: 195). There are many authors writing on this subject, offering varying definitions associated with particular psychological schools of thought. For a detailed discussion on motivation see the work of Pintrich and Schunk (2002).

Motivation can broadly be categorised as either extrinsic (outside the person) or intrinsic (internal to the person). Extrinsic motivation relates to behaviours which occur as a reaction to some external incentive that has some sort of promise of reward, threat of punishment or need for competition or cooperation associated with it. Such motivation requires attainable goals in order for it to be sustained. Intrinsic motivation is linked to an individual's inner drive, often being related to an individual's feelings of self-esteem and to a desire to satisfy personal curiosity. Such motivation provides self-reward for the individual. Gilbert (2002: 2), in his discussions on motivation, asserts that 'motivation is a very misunderstood process . . . carrot and stick may work if you want a classroom full of donkeys, but real motivation comes from within'.

Despite the many definitions of motivation, there is general consensus that motivation is an internal state or condition that serves to activate or energise behaviour and give it direction (Huitt, 2001), and that it is a learned behaviour that will not occur unless energised. Comings et al. (1999: 1) identified in their work, exploring persistence amongst adult learners in America, that:

> a key difference between adult and child learners is that adults choose to participate in educational programmes, whilst children participate because of legal mandates and strong social and cultural forces that identify schooling as the proper 'work' of 'childhood'.

This is interesting in that their work suggests that adults have the freedom to choose to engage in learning programmes. However, Illeris (2003a: 13) provides an alternative perspective in which he suggests that adults do not choose to participate in training programmes, but that:

> Most adult learners approach education in very ambivalent ways. The majority of participants enter the programmes because they are more or less forced to do so, and not because of an inner drive or interest. In practice, they typically develop a variety of psychological defence strategies to avoid learning that challenges their identity and personal ways of thinking, reacting and behaving. In general, it seems to be basically characteristic of adult learning that: adults have very little inclination to really learn something they do not perceive as meaningful for their own life goals; adults in their learning draw on the resources they have; and adults take as much responsibility for their learning as they want to take (if they are allowed to do so).

Illeris argues that the majority of adults attending training programmes at this time are largely doing so because they have to, they are forced to or they have been persuaded to attend, either by employers or authorities, or because the alternative to attendance may result in social and economic marginalisation (Illeris, 2003b).

The findings of Ahrenkiel and Illeris's study (2002) suggest the presence of an ambivalent approach towards education by adults, with motivation being closely associated with employment and employability. Some adults reported attending educational programmes because they wanted to learn something, others reported attending because they had to, with resulting evidence from some of passive resistance and perplexity. Motivations associated with attendance at education programmes appeared to be a mixture of social, personal and technical elements, focusing particularly on the concrete skills they were expected to gain.

While Illeris, discussing the fundamental differences of learning in relation to age (Illeris, 2004), argued that adults want to take personal responsibility in deciding whether they do or do not want to learn, he identifies that, in fact, most adults entering educational institutions have not freely chosen to do so.

Illeris (2003a: 22) concluded that:

the main result of our investigating adult education from the perspective of ordinary learners who are alien to such concepts as lifelong learning and lifelong education is that if it is given to or forced upon participants who have not mentally accepted and internalized a wish or need to acquire the knowledge, skills, attitudes or qualities in question, it will tend to be a waste of human and financial resources.

Reflection

This section provides quite a challenge for those who are either preparing or delivering lifelong learning programmes, and also for those who are being asked to participate in such programmes.

Do you agree that if an individual has been asked to undertake some training as part of their work, they are less or more likely to positively engage in the learning programme because they have not chosen the programme for themselves?

Do you think they are likely to approach the learning with a different motivation than a training programme they have selected for themselves?

What can work-based learning providers do to support and encourage engagement in lifelong learning employment training and skills programmes?

Contemporary application of government policy for work-based learning

Work-based learning, as a strand of lifelong learning, continues to be a strong strand of lifelong learning provision. It is evident from the above discussions that what can be termed as work-based learning is wide ranging. It is further evident from earlier discussions that when people think about lifelong learning, it is often framed within a vocational and economic model. Increasingly, we have seen how policy discussions have returned to the desire to see vocational learning given equal value and status to academic learning, evidenced, for example, through the development of Diplomas (see Chapter 5 on further education).

There has been a simultaneous and parallel discussion throughout successive government discourses of the desire to support the development of a contemporary UK society which is economically active and growing, as well as socially cohesive and responsible. Most recently, these ambitions have been presented in Coalition government policies such as the *Skills for Sustainable Growth* strategy (DBIS, 2010b) and the Big Society (HM Government, 2010).

It is clear that on the completion of compulsory schooling, young adults have very little choice open to them in terms of 'next steps' and many are not motivated to continue to engage in traditional, academic qualifications, preferring instead to explore career options.

Following the rejection by the Coalition government of Diplomas, a central focus of their strategy for lifelong learning going forward is to enable young adults and mature adults alike to either train, or retrain, for a career through the introduction of a new apprenticeship framework. It is this framework that will be presented and explored in this section.

Task

Take some time to review what you already know about apprenticeships:

- What do they involve?
- Who is eligible to engage in apprenticeships?
- What levels of qualification are available?
- Who pays?
- What particular sectors of employment are involved in offering apprenticeships?

Apprenticeships

The policy

Apprenticeships are at the heart of the system of lifelong learning provided by the Coalition government through the *Skills for Sustainable Growth* strategy (DBIS, 2010b). In placing apprenticeships at the heart of the strategy, the government states that:

> They bring together individuals, motivated and working hard to develop themselves; employers, investing in their own success but supporting a programme with wider social, environmental and economic value; and Government, providing public funding and building the prestige and reputation of the programmes.
>
> (DBIS, 2010b: 7)

Through resource initiatives and other interventions, government aims to raise the profile of apprenticeships, increasing the number of available so that by 2014–2015 there will be an annual recruitment of more than 200,000 people starting them. The financial resource invested by government to achieve this ambition was scheduled to be £605 million in 2011–2012 and £648 million in 2012–2012 (DBIS, 2010b: 7).

The apprenticeship agreement

Following the *Apprenticeship, Skills, Children and Learning Act* (ASCL) (Great Britain, 2009), sections 32–36 came into force on 6 April 2012. As a result both parties – employer and learner – are required to enter into an apprenticeship agreement which clearly states that the apprentice will be undertaking an apprenticeship in a particular skills trade or occupation.

Task

This Act pre-dates the *Skills for Sustainable Growth* strategy (DBIS, 2010b) which was developed by the current Coalition government, and was developed under the governance of New Labour.

Download chapter 1 of the Act (http://www.legislation.gov.uk/ukpga/2009/22/part/1/chapter/1) and explore the requirements for those involved in Apprenticeships, from either an employer and learner perspective.

The development of the apprenticeship framework

The development of the new apprenticeship framework will be built through the National Apprenticeship Service (NAS). This organisation, which was launched in 2009, brings together all the key stakeholders involved in the development and delivery of apprenticeships, including Sector Skills Councils, the AELP and employers amongst others, to create 'fit for purpose' and labour-market relevant apprenticeships which are of a high quality and are valued by employers and learners alike. It aims to bring about significant growth in the number of employers who are able to offer apprenticeships.

Crucially, the NAS have been given an 'end to end' responsibility for the delivery of apprenticeships, which includes a web-based vacancy matching system. This online system enables individuals to search and apply for live vacancies and allows employers, and their training providers, to advertise their vacancies to a wide range of interested applicants (NAS, online). As such, the NAS are accountable for achieving the national delivery of targets set down by the government in the *Skills for Sustainable Growth* strategy (DBIS, 2010b), and work to promote apprenticeships, and their value, to employers, learners and the country more widely.

All employers are expected to engage in the development and delivery of apprenticeships, including small and medium employers (SMEs) as well as larger employers.

The curriculum/employment sectors

Apprenticeships are offered across a broad range of employment sectors, including (NAS, online):

- Agriculture, horticulture and animal care
- Business administration and law
- Education and training
- Health, public services and care

- Leisure, travel and tourism
- Arts, media and publishing
- Construction, planning and the built environment
- Engineering and manufacturing
- Information and communication technology
- Retail and commercial enterprise

The delivery model

There are a broad range of delivery models that can be adopted in the delivery of apprenticeships, but what unites them are elements of work experience, applied learning and assessment tasks. However, all elements, whether undertaken at the place of work or in a training environment separate from the place of work, contribute to the working hours of the programme.

The funding

Apprenticeships are supported through funding from the NAS, although it is expected that both employers and learners are willing to contribute to their programme of training. A 'sliding scale' of support has been developed by the NAS, who will cover the training costs of apprentices, dependent on their age, outlined below (NAS, online):

TABLE 6.1 NAS Sliding Scale of Support for Apprentices

AGE	NATIONAL APPRENTICESHIP SERVICE CONTRIBUTION
16–18	Up to 100%
19–24	Up to 50%
25+	Contribution for specific places

All Apprenticeships, in line with the ACSL Act (Great Britain, 2009) are required to be paid in line with the National Minimal Wage regulations (see http://www.direct. gov.uk/en/Employment/Employees/TheNationalMinimumWage for further details regarding these regulations which were brought into force in 1999).

The qualification levels

Historically, apprenticeships have been seen as a model of training for most low-skilled or semi-skilled workers, for example hairdressers, mechanics and office administrators. Often the level of qualification that could be achieved on the completion of an apprenticeship would be Level 2, and hold an equivalency value of five GCSEs. However, under the new framework the government wants employers and participants alike to aspire to both support and deliver apprenticeships that people can achieve at Level 3, with an equivalency value of two or three A levels – considered to be a 'technician' level. In addition, government expects that progression routes will be built into the new apprenticeship frameworks so that participants can enhance their qualifications to engage in Level 4 apprenticeships or access higher education qualifications.

The development of apprenticeship qualifications will take place within the Qualification and Credit Framework (see www.ofqual.gov.uk for a detailed explanation of the framework which exists for all lifelong learning qualifications).

The eligibility

Apprenticeships have traditionally been offered to young people who have just left compulsory schooling at age 16. Under the new framework, it is expected that participants will be drawn from any age group, from 16 upwards. In fact, one of the key aspects of the new apprenticeship framework is the development of apprenticeships specifically for adults aged 25 and over.

The above provides you with an introductory summary of the new apprenticeship framework. This is the heart of current government thinking on developing learning strategies and qualifications that are high quality, fit for purpose and relevant, and can contribute to the economic growth of the contemporary UK. To understand this lifelong learning programme in more detail, you should access the website of the NAS and explore the various elements of the curriculum for those engaging in learning through apprenticeships.

Summary

This chapter has introduced work-based learning as a strand of lifelong learning. It started by exploring the concepts of employment, unemployment and, importantly, employability, which has informed much of the work of many work-based learning providers. We then went on to explore the lifelong learning options for those who are unemployed and in receipt of welfare benefits.

In highlighting some of the key stakeholders involved in contributing to work-based learning programmes, we highlighted the work of Unionlearn, the AELP as well as Sector Skills Councils. In this section we paid particular attention to the notion of choice and motivation when considering adults' engagement in lifelong learning as part of work-based learning. Finally, I have presented the current government policy that informs the way in which work-based learning is articulated through the new apprenticeship framework.

This chapter should have left you with a range of questions and challenges for lifelong learning. For example, should lifelong learning be so focused on economic output? Can such learning be sustained if adults have little choice to engage which may, in turn, compromise their motivation? Is this the best model for enabling people to engage in meaningful learning that can be applied to real working environments?

As a postscript, it is noteworthy that the delivery of teaching qualifications for compulsory schooling is set to change under the Coalition government, with new 'teaching schools' currently being established. It is their ambition that the majority of those who wish to teach in the future will undertake the majority of their training in the learning environment, with less time spent in the classrooms of higher education institutions. It is clear that there are similarities between this model and the model created for apprenticeships. It will be interesting to see how this model develops going forward.

7

Lifelong learning in a prison context

This chapter introduces you to the final strand of lifelong learning provision. What makes this chapter unique is that it starts from the point of the institution (the prison) and the learner (the offender) rather than the learning provider. Lifelong learning can be provided within a prison context across different levels and curricula, and by different providers. However, the reality of lifelong learning provision in this context is strongly regulated and informed by contemporary policy discourse and resources. These areas will inform part of our discussions.

Firstly, the chapter will introduce and explore the range of lifelong learning opportunities available to offenders. In developing this discussion, it will be important to reflect on the terminology associated with lifelong learning in prisons. The policy framework that determines lifelong learning provision in prisons will also be explored, including funding mechanisms.

It is very often the case that discussions around offender lifelong learning focus on male prisoners. This chapter will explore the role of lifelong learning for female as well as male offenders. In concluding, the chapter will explore the role of lifelong learning for this group going forward.

Introduction

It is often surprising to people that lifelong learning programmes are available in an environment that has long been associated with punishment. In this section of the chapter I will explore the types of learning opportunities that offenders can access and how these opportunities are presented, and will then consider how lifelong learning in prisons is organised, managed and funded.

One of the major areas that is often contested, and which can create 'hot' debates, is the merit of providing someone with learning opportunities for free when people on the 'outside' invariably have to pay to access lifelong learning opportunities. A second area of contention is around the area of payment for attending lifelong learning provision – the pros and cons of this matter will also be explored. It is important to acknowledge that such discussions are expected to evoke debate and discussion, and draw out some of your philosophical thinking regarding the role, purpose and value of lifelong learning. It is expected that such debates will challenge you to think about areas such as social justice and equality within the context of lifelong learning provision.

Task

Before we explore lifelong learning provision in prisons for offenders, think about the following questions:

- Do you believe that offenders are in prison in order to pay society for a crime that they have committed and, as such, should not be entitled to access lifelong learning programmes?
- Should offenders be paid to attend lifelong learning programmes?
- What types of lifelong learning programmes, if any, should offenders have to access – academic, vocational?
- What levels should offenders be allowed to study at – Level 1 and 2 only? Degree level?
- Should offenders only be allowed to access learning if there are serving a sentence of 12 months or more? What about offenders who are serving a life sentence?

Trying to develop responses to these questions will provoke some opportunities for you to debate and engage with the following discussions.

Lifelong learning opportunities for offenders

Terminology

Offenders are referred to variously in the literature. Terms that routinely appear include: 'offenders', 'prisoners', 'sentenced prisoners' and 'remand prisoners'. It is worth noting that such terms each have their own connotations and bring with them pictures that can often be stereotypical and dehumanising – and all too often inaccurate. People who are in prison come in all shapes and sizes, from all walks of life and backgrounds, from different ethnic groups and with many different religions. Importantly, offenders are also female, and while you will read later that female offenders only make up 4 per cent of the prison population, they are often the forgotten group when describing offenders.

'Offender' and 'prisoner' are two terms used to described people who are residing in a prison. For the purposes of this chapter, I will uniformly refer to this group as offenders. There are broadly two types of offender – a remand offender and a sentenced offender. A remand offender is a person who is likely to have been charged with committing a criminal offence and is currently awaiting trial. A sentenced offender is a person who has been found guilty of committing a crime and is serving a sentence as punishment for that crime. This distinction is important as remand offenders may or may not be incarcerated in a prison and are not required to undertake any activities, paid or unpaid, during that period of time. Once an individual has been found guilty of a crime and becomes an offender, they can be required to undertake activities, including, for example, drug rehabilitation programmes or paid work such as cleaning.

Lifelong learning opportunities in prisons

Learning in a prison is often greeted with a great deal of tension. All prisons in the UK offer a lifelong learning programme that incorporates both academic (usually underpinned by literacy and numeracy curricula) and vocational training programmes (most often in traditional trades such as building, painting and decorating, as well as catering).

The learning programme is delivered by a lifelong learning provider that has been contracted by the Offender Learning and Skills Service (OLASS) and the Skills Funding Agency (SFA) (see below for discussions on these agencies) to deliver the programme, and so the workforce are not members of the prison service. The level of lifelong learning programmes offered to offenders range from foundation level through to degree level, although these are often dictated by the capability and capacity of the provider, and the funding mechanisms of government.

Traditionally, courses having been provided in the following curriculum areas: literacy and numeracy, social and life skills, and ICT. However, there is a growing demand for the provision of vocational, employment-focused programmes. Programmes are generally offered on a 'workshop' basis and offenders can access a set number of workshops per week, either in the morning or the afternoon during the week. Delivered learning opportunities tend not to be available to offenders at weekends or in the evenings. Generally, offenders get paid a small amount to attend educational programmes.

Policy framework for offender lifelong learning

Lifelong learning, as noted throughout this book, is quite a political term, with different political parties attributing different values, purposes and ambitions to, and for, lifelong learning. When thinking about lifelong learning it is important to remember that the type of learning that is available for the population following compulsory education is significantly influenced by the values and beliefs of different political parties, and this can be seen particularly in the learning provision available to offenders in prisons.

During the period of the New Labour government (1997–2010) the way in which education was provided in prisons was reviewed and revised several times. A series of policy papers influenced this process, leading to the development of structures such as the National Offender Management Service (NOMS) and the OLASS.

National Offender Management Service (NOMS)

The NOMS is an agency of the Ministry of Justice (MoJ). It was created in 2008 and its aim is to support the effective commissioning and delivery of services, in both custodial and community settings. The agency works on behalf of the Probation Service, of which there are 35 Probation Trusts across England and Wales, and HM Prison Service, of which there are 133 in England and Wales. It works with a broad range of partners to deliver programmes and interventions which are specifically designed to encourage a reduction in offending, and lifelong learning programmes are one set of interventions are that commissioned through the NOMS framework.

The Offender Learning and Skills Service (OLASS)

The OLASS began development in 2004 and was launched nationally across the nine regions of England in July 2006. The aim of this service was to organise learning provision for people in prison. The OLASS works on behalf of, and with, the NOMS to commission services on a regional basis across the regions of the UK. For lifelong learning this entails the development of services co-commissioning with the agency responsible for the funding of lifelong learning – the SFA (see below).

The OLASS aims to work with partners to develop lifelong learning opportunities that offer early initial assessments of an individual offender's learning needs, resulting in the development of an individual learning plan that sets out a framework for the offender to achieve their learning goals. The expectation of this model is that offender learners will be able to commence and complete a programme of study, even if they move within the criminal justice system or leave the system and pick up their learning programme through mainstream pathways.

One of the major aims of the development of this service was achieving 'joined up' provision. This is a response to the recognition that very often offenders found themselves transported throughout the prison system, often finding they had to leave learning programmes that had been started or that the programmes they had part-completed had not been recognised, resulting in them having to restart.

Additionally, an ambition of the OLASS is to develop links between learning providers in prisons and learning providers outside prisons, to enable offenders to continue with their learning once released from prison. One of the particular challenges faced here, however, is that offenders are often located in prisons far aware from their home, and so developing good relationships with learning providers near their home can be challenging. A further challenge is the acknowledgement by offenders that they often engage in learning while in prison, but that this is not something they would do outside of the prison environment (O'Grady, 2008).

Skills Funding Agency (SFA)

The SFA coordinates its work through the Department of Business, Innovation and Skills (DBIS), and facilitates the funding and support of lifelong learning across all strands of the sector by responding to and implementing the policy intention of government.

Stakeholders involved in lifelong learning for offenders

The key stakeholders involved in the organisation, management and funding of learning for offenders includes the DBIS, the Department for Education (DfE), the MoJ and the Department for Work and Pensions (DWP), with the main operational focus coming from the SFA, the NOMS (including HM Prison Service and the National Probation Service), the Youth Justice Board (YJB) and the Youth Offending Teams (YOTs), Jobcentre Plus and the Connexions Service.

Offender lifelong learning policy developments

Two key policy documents framed the aims for prison education by the previous New Labour government. Firstly, a consultation document in the form of the Green Paper *Reducing Re-offending Through Skills and Employment* in 2005 (HM Government, 2005). This document sought to identify how the lifelong learning system could better support offenders to gain the knowledge and skills they needed, firstly to obtain and then to sustain employment upon being released from prison.

This was followed, in 2006, with *Reducing Re-offending Through Skills and Employment: Next Steps* (HM Government, 2006). This document responded to, and built on, the 2005 consultation, setting out an ambitious programme of reforms. Three key priority areas were identified (HM Goverment 2006: 3):

■ Engaging employers through the Reducing Re-offending Corporate Alliance (the Reducing Re-offending Corporate Alliance brings together a group of partners to work collaboratively to ensure that the ambitions outlined by the DBIS are operationalised successfully);

■ Building on the new OLASS, including through the campus model (the campus model of delivering learning in prisons enables offenders, through the use of technology, to access learning in a variety of different locations, at different times and in different ways); and

■ Reinforcing the emphasis on skills and jobs in prisons and probation.

These are interesting target areas, showing evidence of an ambition to involve employers in offenders' lifelong learning programmes, and a strong focus on lifelong learning programmes that focus on potential employment opportunities.

Reflection

What are your views on involving employers in the development of lifelong learning programmes for offenders?

Do you think this is likely to result in more employment opportunities for those who have a criminal record?

Should lifelong learning programmes only be focussed on vocational areas? If so, which ones? Why?

The ambitions of government for offender lifelong learning are clearly articulated through these key policy documents. Firstly, they aimed to build a system to ensure that all offenders had the opportunity to evidence, or develop, the necessary underpinning skills seen as essential for active employment and engagement in modern society, namely: literacy, language, numeracy and basic computer skills. In addition, the documents further outlined how the government of the time aimed to enable offenders to have the opportunity to develop work skills that, in turn, would allow them to meet the needs and demands of potential employers in order to gain employment, wherever they settled upon release from custody.

In developing this focused and targeted programme of learning, government highlighted the fact that obtaining and maintaining employment was an instrumental factor in determining whether an individual was likely to reoffend or carry on offending behaviour upon release. Investing in an offender's education, it was felt, was likely to result in reduced recidivism (repeated occurrences of offending), leading to longer-term benefits not only for the offender but for their children and families, the communities in which they live and also wider society.

During the life of the New Labour government, prison education continued to be informed by these documents and these priorities.

Offender learning under the governance of the Coalition

Following the election of the Coalition government, a collaboration between the Conservative and Liberal Democrat parties, in May 2010, the DBIS and the MoJ jointly undertook a review of prisoner education: *Making Prisons Work: Skills for Rehabilitation*. In undertaking this review, the government outlined their intentions to (DBIS, 2011a: 3):

- Be radical and innovative, where it is appropriate to be, in order to make a real contribution to reducing reoffending; and
- Create the conditions that will put a greater focus on local influence to meet more effectively the needs of the labour market and offender learners.

Task

Compare the priorities identified under the two governments, set out below:

Labour government (HM Government, 2006: 3)

- Engaging employers through the Reducing Re-offending Corporate Alliance;
- Building on the new OLASS, including through the campus model;
- Reinforcing the emphasis on skills and jobs in prisons and probation.

Conservative government (DBIS, 2011a: 3)

- Be radical and innovative, where it is appropriate to be, in order to make a real contribution to reducing reoffending; and
- Create the conditions that will put a greater focus on local influence to meet more effectively the needs of the labour market and offender learners.

Can you identify any changes in direction? For example, in the first set of priorities there is evidence of ambitions to develop a range of delivery models for lifelong learning through the OLASS system.

There appears to be a continuing focus on providing lifelong learning opportunities that aim to enhance offenders' employability skills, but there are subtle changes – for example, a move to developing skills that are required for a local labour market.

This policy document results, firstly, from the establishment of an overarching framework for lifelong learning developed by the government and outlined in *Skills for Sustainable Growth* (DBIS, 2010b), which highlights the role and purpose of lifelong learning under their governance, and secondly from the Green Paper produced by the Ministry of Justice in 2010: *Breaking the Cycle: Effective Punishment, Rehabilitation and Sentencing of Offenders* (MoJ, 2010). It is clear from both these documents that decisions regarding lifelong learning opportunities for offenders will be developed to focus on enhancing the skills and aptitudes that will enhance their capacity and capability to secure employment.

Making Prisons Work: Skills for Rehabilitation (DBIS, 2011a) provides a new model for the delivery of lifelong learning in prisons, supported by a focused timetable for its implementation.

The renewed and enhanced focus on the development of offenders' employability skills, both in prison and during probation, requires a reframing of lifelong learning provision, which represents both opportunities and compromises. The enhanced focus on skills development will dictate a curriculum that can provide evidence of achievement through some tangible measure, such as qualifications. This provides real opportunities for offenders to obtain some valuable evidence that they can produce for potential employers. However, such a targeted lifelong learning focus may compromise the opportunity to deliver a curriculum which supports informal learning opportunities that are considered invaluable to enhancing and developing the softer skills equally valued by potential employers, such as confidence and self-esteem.

Following the release of this strategy document for the delivery of lifelong learning in custodial settings, the OLASS and SFA are currently (Spring 2012) undertaking a process of recommissioning lifelong learning services for the offender community. The new contracting regime will enable lifelong learning providers to bid to deliver programmes in custodial settings that meet the requirements of the new framework. The aim is also to incorporate a wider range of training providers, enabling a wide range of expertise to be available to deliver the skills training programmes necessary to achieve the objectives of this new policy framework.

The cost of offending

The cost of reoffending to the country is estimated to be between £9.5 and £13 billion pounds per year (DBIS, 2011a: 5). One of the major reasons given for reoffending behaviour has been the inability of offenders to obtain and maintain employment as a result of a changing labour market, moving from one which had employment opportunities for those with low or no skills, to one which is increasingly based on a knowledge economy, requiring individuals to have a basic education as a minimum, including literacy, numeracy and ICT skills which can be demonstrated through the achievement of qualifications.

Lifelong learning for local demand

One of the key differences identified in the new model of lifelong learning for offenders is the ambition to create programmes which are responsive to local influences, particularly in terms of employment skills gaps. While such a focus provides the opportunity for lifelong learning provision to be targeted to meet the needs of the local economy, it is noteworthy that offenders are often not located in a prison which is local to their resettlement area. Even though offenders are likely to have the opportunity to develop transferable employment skills while engaging in lifelong learning programme, they are not necessarily always going to be directly useful to the employment market of their resettlement area. This presents a challenge to lifelong learning providers in terms of identifying the labour market that they are tasked to influence.

The objective of the strategy is clearly stated: to put in place a lifelong learning system that is responsive (to the needs of the labour market) and flexible (to be able to adapt to changing labour market situations and demands). However, the challenge here is to be able to build a curriculum that is not only able to meet the needs of the labour market, but also enables an individual offender to meet his personal learning goals and objectives.

Quality of lifelong learning in prisons

Currently Ofsted (Office for Standards in Education, Children's Services and Skills) are responsible for ensuring that lifelong learning provision is provided to offenders by providers working within their inspection framework. However, ensuring the quality of lifelong learning provision in prison is challenging. One of the biggest challenges that prisons face is the regular, quickly planned movement of offenders between prisons, undertaken for a variety of often very valid reasons. However, this can have significant consequences for those undertaking lifelong learning programmes. Examples could be that the receiving prison does not deliver the programme the offender was studying; the offender is unable to evidence their engagement in the programme; that any paperwork that evidences engagement in learning takes time to 'catch up' with the offender. Any break in an offender's learning programme is likely to influence their ability to be able to complete their programme of study successfully. The quality of lifelong learning provision in prisons is an area of renewed focus within this new policy.

Reflection

Do you think that lifelong learning programmes in prison should be required to be delivered to the same standard as other programmes across the sector?

How would you like to see such provision monitored?

Funding of lifelong learning for offenders

Funding for lifelong learning provision is a contentious issue. The majority of lifelong learning provided for offenders has been free, with only a small minority of offenders contributing to the cost of higher-level education, such as undergraduate programmes. The same funding model is applied to offenders accessing lifelong learning in the same way as any other member of the population.

What makes lifelong learning for offenders in prison somewhat unique is that often offenders are paid to attend their lifelong learning programmes. As we have noted earlier, remand prisoners are not required to undertake any activity while being held in custody, but sentenced or convicted offenders are often required to undertake tasks. These are often in the form of some low skilled work for which they receive payment. While such payment is minimal, it does provide offenders with an income from which they can buy incidental items – for example, coffee, chocolate or cigarettes – or save up for items such as electrical goods.

Offenders who choose to undertake lifelong learning opportunities generally receive a payment, although this is usually much less than they would receive for engaging in other employment workshops. However this model, under the auspices of the new policy, will be reviewed, particularly in light of the newly introduced further education loan system where adults will be expected to contribute to the cost of their lifelong learning programmes at Levels 2 and 3.

Timetable for implementation

The deadline given in the strategy for implementation of the policy is August/September 2012. This is ambitious as it requires the commissioning of new contracts with new services, as noted earlier. The key difference in negotiating new contracts will be that providers will be required to link the lifelong learning outcome achievements of the offender learner with opportunities for employment outcomes. This presents additional challenges for lifelong learning providers in delivering these outcomes, as some offenders may be serving relatively long sentences, some may not resettle in the local community of the prison where they have served their sentence, and offenders are likely to face significantly more barriers to achieving employment than the general population.

Curriculum offer and delivery model

It is clear that the new learning offer for offenders will focus on a vocational curriculum offer but it will also incorporate intensive literacy and numeracy provision as needed. It is expected that a range of delivery models will be used to enable offenders to engage in lifelong learning programmes, and it is expected that providers will draw on and use the virtual campus (a security protected virtual learning environment) available in custodial settings.

Informal learning for offenders

While the role of adult and community learning is considered in the new framework for offenders, and there is recognition in the policy of the value of such informal learning opportunities, particularly in terms of motivating and engaging reticent or less confident individuals in learning – supporting mental well-being and developing confidence and self-esteem – there is little opportunity for offenders to engage in such provision. It is expected that only offenders serving longer sentences are likely to engage in such activity, although again it is unclear how such learning opportunities may be made available through the new contracting formula.

Offender lifelong learning under the new policy framework

The challenge for this new policy, and the opportunity, are the same – the drive to develop offenders' skills to enable their employability potential in mainstream society. Such a focus is a particularly narrow one, and while there is merit in this approach, there are nevertheless questions that should be asked. For example, how are offenders being supported to develop their 'social capital'? The focus on skills detracts from some of the wider and, arguably, more important areas of lifelong learning which could potentially be missed – those informal learning opportunities that provide the chance for individuals to really develop their confidence and self-esteem. It is with this in mind that it is important to consider the reasons behind the existence of prison.

Profile of an offender

Offenders are often profiled in the media as young male men who are sentenced to serve time in prison for a period determined by the judicial system. Typically, offenders are described as black, young (between 18 and 24), uneducated (i.e. no qualifications), from disadvantaged backgrounds (low socio-economic scale), who are often already known to institutions of the state, such as welfare services, including childcare services, and the criminal justice service.

The total population of offenders in prison across England and Wales sits at just under 90,000, with the current number, as of June 2012, at 81,925 males and 4,123 females (ONS, online). Of that number, approximately 80 per cent of those held in custody were 'sentenced males aged 18 or older', with a further 14 per cent being recorded as on remand. It is also noteworthy that females make up just 4 per cent of the total prison population.

The characteristics of an offender, outlined by the House of Commons Library (2012) reveals that 47 per cent of male sentenced offenders and 50 per cent of female sentenced offenders had run away from home as a child, compared to 10 per cent of the general population. Furthermore, over 25 per cent of offenders had been taken into care as a child compared to 2 per cent of the population. Additionally, 43 per cent of offenders had a family member who had been convicted of a criminal offence, with 35 per cent having a family member who had been incarcerated. Interestingly, 81 per cent of offenders were unmarried prior to their imprisonment, which is almost twice that of the general population.

In terms of educational background, half of male and one-third of female sentenced offenders had been excluded from school at some point during their compulsory education, with half of male and seven out of ten female offenders holding no qualifications. Two-thirds of offenders have numeracy skills that are at or below the level expected of an 11 year old, with half have a reading ability and 82 per cent having a writing ability at or below this level.

When an offender's employment history is reviewed, two-thirds of offenders were unemployed in the four weeks before their imprisonment and nearly three-quarters of offenders were in receipt of state benefits immediately prior to entering prison.

From the above profile, it becomes apparent that for many offenders, partial education has resulted in their limited capacity to access, or sustain, meaningful employment which has, for some, resulted in offending behaviour. Given this profiling, the current government's policy of developing an interventionist strategy which seeks to give offenders access to lifelong learning programmes that provides them with the opportunity to develop their educational capacity, and their employability, is a reasonable one which may, in turn, enable offenders to obtain employment upon release and so prevent a cycle of reoffending.

What is prison for: retribution or recidivism?

The purpose of prison is an ongoing debate both within the criminal justice system and in society more broadly. Some members of society might argue that prison should be used as a punishment for going against societal rules. For others, time spent in prison should be used as an opportunity for rehabilitation, by ensuring that prisoners develop the capacity to participate in mainstream society through being offered opportunities to: reform their behaviours; understand the impact of their criminal behaviours on society; review their health and become no longer dependent on drugs or alcohol; and review their employability skills, develop vocational skills and enhance their qualification profiles.

While the purpose of prison sits at a tension point been retribution (punishment for crime undertaken) and recidivism (reoffending), it is acknowledged in the literature (see for example Schuller, 2009) that an increased educational capacity is likely to result is less criminal activity and reoffending.

Task

What do you think prison is for?

Download: Schuller, T. (2009) *Crime and Lifelong Learning, IFLL Thematic Paper 5*, http://www.niace.org.uk/lifelonglearninginquiry/docs/IFLL-Crime.pdf.

This will help you to explore the role of lifelong learning opportunities in prison and how that informs the purpose and role of prisons in contemporary UK society.

Women in prison

While women represent only 4 per cent of the total prison population, this equates to approximately 4,200 females (House of Commons Library, 2012) as of March 2012. Lifelong learning opportunities for women offenders is provided within a lifelong learning programme framework that is the same across all custodial settings. However, it is worth considering the specific challenges faced many female offenders.

Women's lifelong learning opportunities in prison

A seminal report that influenced the planning, management and organisation of women's education in prison was published in 2007 – *The Corston Report* (Home Office, 2007). This report was the culmination of an inquiry undertaken by Baroness Jean Corston in 2006, which reviewed the experiences of women with particular vulnerabilities in the criminal justice system. The report made multiple recommendations, but an overarching conclusion of the inquiry regarded the need to develop a radically different approach to women offenders that drew appropriately on multiple partners to develop an integrated women-centred response to them as offenders.

Using a qualitative methodology, interviewing in excess of 200 individuals, Corston explored the range of challenges that incarcerated women faced, not only in terms of the personal impact that incarceration has but also the wider effects on family networks and particularly any children they have caring responsibilities for. In undertaking her review, Corston identified three categories of vulnerability faced by women who are incarcerated following conviction: domestic, personal and socio-economic factors. Her report concluded that for many women, placing them in prison to serve their sentence once being found guilty of criminal activity was inappropriate – instead the majority of women should be offered more community-based support.

Interestingly, the review identified an absence of lifelong learning opportunities to support the development of what was termed 'emotional literacy', from which it was argued all learning should commence. This observation recognised the need for a curriculum that was broader than the achievement of just literacy and numeracy qualifications, and suggested institutions should consider the development of more informal learning opportunities, or non-accredited learning, such as programmes which focus on self-confidence. Corston recommended that life-skills learning 'should be given a much higher priority within the education, training and employment pathway and women must be individually assessed to ensure that their needs are met' (Home Office, 2007: 8).

The report was welcomed by the New Labour government, who accepted some of its recommendations either in full or in part.

Task

Download a copy of the government response to the *Corston Report* (MoJ, 2007):

- Explore the government response to the recommendations.
- Of the 43 recommendations made, consider how many were accept in full or in part and how many were rejected. Do you agree with the decision making?
- Do you think anything has changed in the last five years since this response?

Interestingly, the new policy that informs and frames offending for the future does not distinguish between male or female offenders, and considers them as one group.

Task

Do you think treating male and female offenders as one group, rather than considering their lifelong learning needs and priorities differently is reasonable?

Role of lifelong learning for offenders going forward

What is evident from the discussions above is that the role of offender learning is a contentious one. For some, lifelong learning opportunities should not be made available at all – prisons should be regarded as punitive – while for others in society (and the current focus of lifelong learning programmes in prison), time spent in prison should be about developing the knowledge and skills necessary to be able to contribute economically in society upon release from prison through employment. Lifelong learning then can be identified as a framework through which offenders can be challenged to reflect on their behaviours and work towards changing such behaviours and attitudes (Schuller, 2009).

Lifelong learning can contribute to both the social and economic well-being of society, and as such this should be reflected in the lifelong learning offer made to offenders, whether in prison or serving their sentence in the community. However, it is important to recognise that there are many challenges to be faced in the effective delivery of learning opportunities and engagement of offenders.

The first issue is the movement of offenders. As might be expected, offenders have very little control over their movements and can be moved from one prison to another with little or no notice. If an offender is in prison on remand they may be required to attend court, or receive visits from their legal team; they may find themselves released from court without returning to prison; or they may have health demands that require appointments with the health staff of the prison.

Such movements require a lot of logistical planning on the part of the prison, without the time or opportunity to involve the lifelong learning department. As such, offenders may find themselves either missing learning opportunities, moving prisons without any evidence of the learning they have been engaged in, or being released from the prison system without any evidence of their engagement and achievement in their lifelong learning programme.

The movement of offenders between prisons has been an area of focus and has resulted in the development of a 'passport' that can either travel with an offender as they move through the system or 'catch up' with them. Additionally, the development of a virtual learning campus, and a plan to enable data sharing between prisons is likely to result in the closer tracking of individual offenders, learning programmes, goals and achievements to date.

The length of an offender's sentence also influences the opportunity for offenders to engage in lifelong learning programmes. If an offender is sentenced to a period of less than 12 months there are fewer opportunities for them to engage in a meaningful programme of learning that will fulfil the ambitions of the new policy direction for offender learning and, importantly, this does not appear to be considered within the strategy document. This is a crucial missing element of discussion, and equality of opportunity should be given a higher priority and transparency in discussing the future of lifelong learning for offenders.

As noted previously, for individuals who are on remand or awaiting sentence there is no obligation for them to engage in any activity in prison, including lifelong learning. This is a cause for concern as opportunities may be missed to work with individuals to develop their capacity to reintegrate into society effectively.

There continues to be a need to ensure that staff – both lifelong learning staff and prison staff – are able to support offenders in the development of their skills, particularly literacy and numeracy. This is challenging for staff that have very different job descriptions and targets. As the new model for delivering lifelong learning in prisons evolves, and changes are made to the requirements for staff working in the lifelong learning sector (see discussions regarding the lifelong learning workforce in Chapter 2), it will be necessary for contracted providers of lifelong learning to ensure that the common ambition to support offenders is achieved between both sets of staff.

A further aim of the new framework is to ensure that offenders who have been identified as having learning difficulties or disabilities can access the support they need to enable them to persist, progress and achieve with their lifelong learning programme. While it is acknowledged that it is the responsibility of any lifelong learning provider to make anticipatory arrangements for a broad range of learning needs and make reasonable adjustments, the likely high levels of support that will be needed by this particular group is likely to create some challenges in terms of resources. It will also be necessary for providers to consider issues of disclosure and support when developing lifelong learning opportunities for offenders, particularly if learning is planned across the prison environment to incorporate vocational learning.

Further challenges likely to be faced by providers include the opportunity to enable offenders to progress with their learning beyond Level 2. While it is well recorded in the literature (see for example Brooks et al., 2001; Rice, 1999) that offenders have a significantly higher incidence of dyslexia and lower levels of literacy compared to the general population, there are a small number of offenders for whom Level 3 learning programmes and beyond should be made available. Providing appropriate mechanisms through which such learning demands can be met is likely to require creative and innovative ways of working, perhaps in partnership with organisations with whom new working relationships will need to be established.

The contemporary measure through which learning is articulated as successful appears to be through qualification achievement. However, it is noteworthy than many offenders may have engaged in lifelong learning programmes and achieved a number of identified goals from their individual learning plans without actually obtaining a qualification. There is a missed opportunity here for the providers of lifelong learning to utilise mechanisms to allow such achievements to be acknowledged.

Summary

The provision of learning opportunities for offenders is problematic. On the one hand, prison is seen as a site of punishment, where people lose their liberty for a determined period of time as a result of being found guilty of committing a criminal offence. On the other hand, prison can be seen as a site of opportunity to reduce recidivism – to provide people with the opportunity to develop the knowledge and skills necessary to be able to be both economically and socially effective members of society. The new model of delivery of lifelong learning provision in prisons certainly affords the opportunity to develop a stronger human capital stock, but potentially limits the capacity for society capital redevelopment, particularly in areas such as self-esteem and confidence.

The challenges of delivering lifelong learning continue to be tested, for all of the reasons we have discussed above, including the movement of prisoners, the range of curricula available, the funding support, and the challenge of learning being delivered in prisons operated privately outside of the control of the state or Ofsted regimes.

The ambitions and aspirations associated with lifelong learning are intrinsically good ones, but the focus on economic and employment outcomes may stifle the potential to provide more informal learning opportunities, and so there may be missed opportunities.

One of the major areas for discussion is whether education in prison really has economic and social value, and whether it is in fact a key element in the ambition to reintegrate offenders into mainstream society, or whether it is just a mechanism that can be used to 'pass the time'. Questions will always be asked regarding who should pay for prison education and why, what types of curricula should offenders have access to, and should they really be paid to engage in learning. This is an area for you to think about as you go on to explore in more detail the purpose, role and value of lifelong learning in contemporary society for offenders.

8

The future of lifelong learning

This chapter considers lifelong learning for the future – how the sector may be taken forward in order to provide a comprehensive lifelong learning framework; one which offers opportunities for the population to engage in lifelong learning that is socially just and responsive to the needs and demands of the population generally, as well as the economy specifically. Additionally, it will consider the lifelong learning offer of the contemporary UK within a global framework, and question whether lifelong learning is meeting the needs and demands of a global marketplace.

To enable the discussion, I have framed the following key questions:

- What does a new government mean for the evolution of lifelong learning in contemporary UK society?
- Who will be the beneficiaries of policy changes, and who will be the losers?
- How can lifelong learning in the UK be positioned within a global market?

Implications of the Coalition government

A change of political governance strongly influences the direction of the lifelong learning sector in contemporary UK society, although this is often subtle.

During the 13-year lifetime of the Labour government (1997–2010) lifelong learning policy moved from: an equal focus on skills to enable people to engage in society both socially and economically (during the first half of their governance, see for example policy documents including the *Skills for Life* strategy, DfEE (2001a)); to an increasingly narrow focus on skills development that would enhance the economic capability of the country in a increasingly competitive global marketplace, requiring that employees hold particular skills to meet productivity demands (during the second half of their governance, see for example Leitch (2006)).

These two documents were key to determining the role, focus and purpose of lifelong learning during the lifetime of the New Labour government, demonstrated through frameworks which focused funding directly towards those curriculum areas that would enable government to achieve its ambitions for the directional growth of society.

In May 2010 a new Liberal Democrat–Conservation Coalition government was established. The direction of contemporary UK lifelong learning is being given its direction and focus from this combination of political influence to determine and inform the direction of societal growth. It is evident from the guiding strategy document – *Skills for Sustainable Growth* (DBIS, 2010b) – that economic growth lies at the heart of their focus and framing of the lifelong learning sector, across all strands, by placing apprenticeships at the heart of this flagship strategy.

Funding is transparently directed towards curricula that have either an employability focus, or employment outcomes. Throughout this book we have seen examples of this drive to enable unemployed adults to develop employability skills – for example, the Work Programme and the creation of the new contracting framework for offenders which ensures that the curriculum offer is closely associated with employment outcomes. However, it is important to acknowledge the continued commitment of the government to adult and community learning opportunities. This is demonstrated through their support for the development of Community Learning Trusts (DBIS, 2012). The ambition set out in this strategy is to support the creation of community groups to enhance social capital development.

The changes to the lifelong learning framework set out in the *Skills for Sustainable Growth* strategy documents (DBIS, 2010b) are framed through three key concepts – fairness, freedom and responsibility. Under this framework, the government sets out the expectations placed on each member of society to take responsibility for their lifelong learning journey, by contributing financially to the cost of their learning programme. There is also acknowledgment that there are some members of society who may be less able contribute financially to their learning programme, and so financial support will be made available.

Such an approach to funding lifelong learning – requiring individuals to contribute to Level 2 and Level 3 learning from age 24 onwards – is a new model, and one which has been scrutinised and challenged. This model makes each individual accountable for their own lifelong learning journey. There is an implicit assumption that if you invest in your learning, you are likely to be rewarded with economic success and prosperity. Indeed, there is research from the Office of National Statistics that supports the fact that those who achieve a degree are able to obtain employment that is substantially more economically rewarding than those who do not obtain a higher education degree. However, there is research yet to be done to confirm a similar outcome for lower levels of qualification.

This individual model of engagement in learning through self-funding does challenge both the role and responsibility of the employer in supporting continuing professional development, or the role of society in supporting and enabling the most vulnerable members of society. The challenge of employer responsibility is met by the high focus and central development of apprenticeships. Through the development of apprenticeships, employers are placed in a position of influence in terms of the direction of qualifications and funding of programmes that aid their business. Work-based learning has increasingly been seen as playing a crucial role in lifelong learning at all levels, from Level 2 basic apprenticeships through to graduate and postgraduate qualifications, including the introduction of new teacher training models. Employers can also support individual engagement in lifelong learning programmes with a vocational focus through financial support, although this is not mandatory.

The challenge then is in supporting members of society who are seen to be the most vulnerable, who could be identified as most at risk from exclusion or marginalisation from society. It is these members of society who are, arguably, protected by the new strategy (DBIS, 2010b), as it provides continuing support to such groups so that they can achieve initial qualifications at Level 1 and below, particularly in literacy and numeracy qualifications.

It is clear then, that any government strongly influences the direction and focus of lifelong learning provision in contemporary UK society, and it is perhaps surprising how lifelong learning has become a central policy tool that strongly influences the way in which society is constructed and reproduced, and how it evolves. As with the introduction of new policy frameworks, questions arise regarding who might benefit most from the change in policy direction, and who may feel compromised. It is this question that is considered next.

Who will be the beneficiaries and losers?

The lifelong learning policy changes introduced by the Coalition government appear to support all members of society. Indeed, it is clear that government has a strong commitment to social equality and social justice through the publication of *Social Justice: Transforming Lives* (HM Government, 2012). This document sets out the government's ambitions for social justice for all members of UK society. Social justice, in this framework, is the ambition to tackle poverty and multiple disadvantages. The commitment to social justice is articulated through the introduction of a series of early intervention activities.

Lifelong Learning as an intervention strategy can be seen as having the potential to influence the life chances of many individuals who show a need for support, through targeted curricula. Groups include (HM Government, 2012):

- Lone-parent families, where there is evidence that 28 per cent of children live in relative poverty;

- Low-income families, where there is evidence that children who are eligible for free school meals are more than four times as likely as those not eligible for free school meals to be permanently excluded from school;

- Workless households, of which there are currently around 3.9 million;

- Individuals who experience substance dependence, either drug or alcohol. 80 per cent of heroin and crack cocaine users in England are in receipt of working-age benefits. There are also 1.1 million dependent drinkers;

- Those in debt, with approximately 165,000 households using illegal money lenders – 6 per cent of households in the most deprived areas; and

- Offenders, of whom 24 per cent report being taken into care, and 53 per cent not growing up on a household with both natural parents.

This ambition is evidenced in the *Skills for Sustainable Growth* strategy (DBIS, 2010b), through the continued commitment to supporting individuals who wish to engage in lifelong learning who are seen as most vulnerable and at risk of being marginalised or excluded from society. Such interventions include the creation of Community Trusts, and programmes for those who are identified as not in education, employment or training (NEET).

It could be argued therefore that those who are identified as the most in need, and exposed to multiple disadvantages, are rightly supported by the current strategic approach to lifelong learning programmes. However, there are two areas of contention – the role of lifelong learning for all member of society, and the direction and focus of lifelong learning on economic prosperity: arguably the losers within this new policy framework.

Lifelong learning has over recent decades been focused on supporting members of society who are, arguably, the most marginalised from mainstream society, who have limited capacity to draw on social or cultural capital and have restricted capability in terms of economic capital. There is an increasingly narrow focus on engagement in lifelong learning programmes that offer economic gain, through employability or employment outcomes, and this is most clearly demonstrated in the funding of particular curricula and the increasing profile of vocational programmes, including apprenticeships.

However, this focus, in and of itself, limits lifelong learning programmes that appeal to all members of society and may create some 'losers' as a result. For example, there is a whole community of older-aged adults who may benefit from lifelong learning programmes for social interaction purposes, as well as for skills development. There has been much research undertaken on behalf of the inquiry into the future of lifelong learning (Schuller and Watson, 2009) that demonstrates the benefits of engagement in lifelong learning to health and well-being – for example, the benefits to older-aged adults of engaging in digital learning programmes to avoid them becoming isolated from a society that increasingly undertakes its business through online technology, including banking, travel arrangements and shopping. Also, there may be challenges for members of society who would like to engage in learning to fulfil personal interests, as providers are increasingly focusing their provision in line with government guidelines and are less able to provide more informal lifelong learning programmes as they are non-credit bearing and are not linked directly to qualification outcomes.

Task

Identify any other groups who may be seen as 'losers' as result of the new lifelong learning framework set out by the Coalition government.

Consider whether this is really a challenge for our society. It is right that government funding and focus is directed to those members of society who are most disadvantaged? Is this really representative of equality, or social justice?

How would you build a lifelong framework that offered opportunities for all members of society, equally?

Lifelong learning in a global market

Lifelong learning in the contemporary UK can be clearly positioned within an economic, functionalist model which is responding to the challenges of economic markets, while also ambitiously trying to maintain support for social cohesion, but is this the case for all countries? It is important to consider how lifelong learning in the UK is positioned in an increasingly linked global market framework.

The OECD was established in 1961 to promote policies to improve both the economic and social well-being of people around the world. Through this forum governments can work together, sharing their experiences and seeking solutions to common challenges or problems. The OECD works with governments to understand and articulate the economic and social drivers that lead to change, analysing and comparing data on global trade and investment, and using this analysis to predict future trends. One of their key areas of focus is to compare education systems and question their effectiveness in preparing people for their lives, both now and for the future, and subsequently make recommendations for development.

The concept of lifelong learning as a global educational strategy emerged approximately three decades ago, through the efforts of the OECD with UNESCO and the Council of Europe. This focus emerged through the recognition that while it was documented that individuals learn throughout their lifetime, the majority of learning opportunities were largely located in the early phases of life and dominated by formal education. The above organisations articulated a need to ensure that 'second chance' opportunities to engage in learning were made available. Lifelong learning, from an OECD perspective, encompasses all learning endeavours over a person's life, not just recurrent or adult education.

When exploring lifelong learning for all, Larsen and Istance (2001) identified that the role of education could often be described as 'double-edged' – being successful in one area while simultaneously being accused of social selectivity. The role of lifelong learning, they argued, was to work to increasingly focus on achieving equality of opportunity throughout peoples' lives. They asserted that the ambition of all countries should be to make lifelong learning opportunities available for all, ensuring that lifelong learners are not only those who have already done well in initial education.

There is clear evidence from the OECD that participation in lifelong learning tends to follow the patterns of initial education, which maintains the potential divide between those who have had constructive experiences of initial schooling and those who have not. Larsen and Istance (2001) argued that the public strategies of countries for adult learning should be targeted at those who have, for whatever reason, missed out on early educational opportunities. Strategically, they state that countries should set clear goals, targets and priorities for lifelong learning against which progress could be monitored, ensuring that equality becomes an integral aspect of both the policy and the practice of delivery.

The OECD's aim is to monitor countries' performance in providing lifelong learning programmes. However, they state that their work is compromised by limited comparable data between countries. One of the reasons given for this is the nature of lifelong learning itself. Provision in some countries lies outside of formal structures and focuses predominantly on lifelong learning opportunities that are informal. That said, the OECD records that over the last three decades countries have made impressive gains in providing education and training opportunities for their populations. While much of this progress has been made in ensuring universal secondary education, some countries record a nearly 50 per cent engagement in tertiary education by their population, with a significant percentage of adults also participating in some type of formal training. However, it is also evident that two-thirds of adults across most countries do not participate in organised learning activities, particularly if there is little participation by older adults.

Lifelong learning as a concept has largely been embraced by countries at a political level. However, the development of policy responses for its implementation is inconsistent. The OCED offers a lifelong learning framework that offers a focus for countries in identifying priority areas for policy reform. The five systemic features suggested are:

- Improving access, quality and equity;
- Ensuring foundation skills for all;
- Recognising all forms of learning, not just formal courses of study;
- Mobilising resources, rethinking resource allocation across all sectors, settings and over the life cycle; and
- Ensuring collaboration among a wide range of partners.

By developing a lifelong learning framework that responds to the above features, the OCED argues that it can play an important role in breaking cycles of disadvantage, enabling social cohesion and providing conditions for economic development. Crucially, the OECD asserts that lifelong learning programmes should be built that are contextual to the adult learner, and provide choice and control over the learning being engaged in.

There is some evidence then that the UK's response to, and implementation of, lifelong learning policies and interventions are in line with the OECD's lifelong learning framework. In fact, the UK can be said to be leading the way in committing to lifelong learning policy and supporting its implementation through a range of strategy interventions and funding resources. The government have linked lifelong learning quality to the Ofsted education quality framework in place in the UK; have responded to the demand for a quality delivery through the enforcement of the development of a professionalised workforce; and have developed a suite of qualifications to enable lifelong learners to evidence their engagement and achievement in lifelong learning programmes.

It is clear that countries provide varying lifelong learning programmes. While some see lifelong learning as a largely informal activity which is peripheral to the educational provision of the country, others link lifelong learning to programmes that can enhance employment, and others to social, informal learning. Comparing lifelong learning provision in the UK with other countries is an important area of consideration, whether that comparison is with other developed countries, other continents or developing countries.

Conclusion

As you will have to identified, through delving into this introductory text, lifelong learning is complex and messy. Some argue that lifelong learning refers to learning throughout the life course, others frame lifelong learning as learning in the post-16 sector. Some argue that it is second-chance learning, and others about learning for work or learning that is not accredited, or, contradictorily, learning that is facilitated and accredited.

Through this text you have been introduced to a range of debates and discussions around lifelong learning in the contemporary UK. You have been introduced to a swath of changing terminology used to discuss, explore and focus lifelong learning – in fact, we should now be calling the sector the further education and skills sector! You have been introduced to the various locations in which lifelong learning can be accessed and you have been introduced to some of the learners who are likely to engage in lifelong learning opportunities. It is important to remember, however, that this is an introductory text and should be treated as such. There is much more to discuss, for example: the role of technology in lifelong learning; the role of early years and compulsory education in creating a culture of lifelong learning; whether demography influences the opportunities to engage in learning; and lifelong learning as it happens in other countries.

What is clear is that, despite the different ways of describing and explaining lifelong learning, it plays a significant and fundamental role in our educational offering to society. Lifelong learning allows and enables our society to be socially aware and just, providing opportunities for all, equally, to engage in a range of learning opportunities for either individual, social or economic gain, or more broadly for national prosperity and social cohesion.

Lifelong learning should be seen to provide opportunities to support the social and economic potential of both the individual and society more widely. By prioritising and focusing on one type of learning over another, there is the potential to provide a skewed offer that does not cater for the needs of all strata of society.

This book has provided you with the opportunity to develop a good understanding of the underpinning framework that supports lifelong learning in contemporary UK society. You will have developed an awareness of the potential role and purpose of lifelong learning and the ability to question why some learning appears to be privileged over other types of learning. Additionally, you can debate whether lifelong learning really can be one of the key measures used to demonstrate the creation of a more just society, and the role of politics in framing lifelong learning.

What is clear is that lifelong learning is a concept with a long history that has informed social and economic policy for decades, and will continue to do so as society evolves. Lifelong learning as a concept is difficult to pin down to a single definition, and it means different things to different audiences and stakeholders – whether policy-makers, employers or learners. What lifelong learning has the potential to achieve is very unique. Lifelong learning has the opportunity to be transformative, and provides a framework through which real social justice for all elements of society can be achieved. In order for this aspiration to be accomplished however, lifelong learning needs to be understood for what it is: a complex, multifaceted set of learning opportunities that aims to meet all our societies' needs.

Notes

1 Introduction to lifelong learning

1. Success is a very abstract term with many meanings. Value is, for example, often applied in our society to qualification success. Possession of particular success can lead to, for example, social status or higher economic return. Indeed, much research has been done to evidence a correlation between qualification attainment and economic return. It is important to remember, however, that success is a very individual account of achievement, and failure in one person's eyes can be the pinnacle of success in another. An individual can be identified as very successful in one area of their lives while at the same time being seen as very unsuccessful in another; for example holding a responsible job while experiencing an unsuccessful personal relationship. Within the context of this discussion, success is identified as a government indicator that closely associates engagement in learning that results in a qualification outcome as having the potential to yield an economic return to the country through potential to gain, maintain and enhance employment opportunities.
2. Types of learning – formal, informal and non-formal – will be discussed in more detail in Chapter 3 on Adult and Community Learning.

2 The development of lifelong learning in the UK: The policy context

1. Social justice is a term used widely in the literature to describe a society in which all members have equal opportunities to access social institutions and organisations, and contribute equally to the creation of a society that treats its members with fairness.
2. The term 'level' is used to refer to the position of a qualification with a qualification 'hierarchy'. For example: Level 1 qualifications are described as the bank of qualifications that are equivalent to GCSE grades D–F; Level 2, GCSE grades A*–C; Level 3, A-Level grades A–E; Levels 4–6, undergraduate degrees; and Levels 7–8, postgraduate degrees.

3 Adult and community learning

1. The term 'strata' refers to a 'range', and strata are often explained as 'positions on a ladder'. A stratum of which we are most commonly aware of is the social class into which people are 'slotted' – a particular location in a society's strata.

References

Age Concern (2012) *Introducing Another World: Older People and Digital Inclusion*. Available from: www.ageconcern.org.uk. Accessed August 2012.

Ahrenkiel, A. and Illeris, K. (2002) 'Adult Education Between Emancipation and Control' in Illeris, K., *Adult Education in the Perspective of the Learners*, Copenhagen: Roskilde University Press, pp. 116–36.

Armitage, A., Bryant, R., Dunnill, R., Hammersley, M., Hayes, D., Hudson, A. and Lawes, S. (2003) *Teaching and Training in Post-compulsory Education*, 2nd edition, Maidenhead: Open University Press.

Atkin, C. (2000) 'Lifelong Learning Attitudes to Practice in the Rural Context: A Study Using Bourdieu's Perspective of Habitus', *International Journal of Lifelong Education*, Vol. 19, No. 3: 253–65.

Atkin, C., Rose, A. and Shier, R. (2005) *Provision Of, and Learner Engagement With, Adult Literacy, Numeracy and ESOL Support in Rural England: A Comparative Case Study*, London: National Research and Development Centre.

Bauman, Z. (1997) 'Universities: Old, New and Different' in Smith, A. and Webster, F. (eds) *The Postmodern University? Contested Visions of Higher Education in Society*, Buckingham: Society for Research into Higher Education and Open University Press.

Bill, D. (1998) 'The Dearing Inquiry into United Kingdom Higher Education and the Role of Lifelong Learning in the Learning Society' in *Research in Post-compulsory Education*, Vol. 3, No. 3: 279–6.

Bourdieu, P. (1977) *Outline of a Theory of Practice*, (trans. Nice, R.), Cambridge: Cambridge University Press.

Bourdieu, P. (1993) *Sociology in Question*, London: Sage Publications Ltd.

Bourdieu, P. (1997) 'The Forms of Capital' (trans. Nice, R.) in Halsey, A. H., Lauder, H., Brown, P. and Wells, A. S. (eds.) *Education, Culture, Economy and Society*, Oxford: Oxford University Press, pp. 46–58.

Bourdieu, P. (1998) *Acts of Resistance*, Cambridge: Polity Press.

Bourdieu, P. and Passeron, J-C. (1977) *Reproduction in Education, Society and Culture*, 2nd edition (trans. Nice, R.), London: Sage.

Bowman, H., Burden, T. and Konrad, J. (2000) *Successful Futures? Community Views on Adult Education and Training*, York: Publishing Services.

Brooks, G., Giles, K., Harman, J., Kendall, S., Rees, F. and Whittaker, S. (2001) *Assembling the Fragments: A Review of Research on Adult Basic Skills*, London: Department for Education and Employment.

Browne, J. (2010) *Securing a Sustainable Future for Higher Education in England*, Available from: www.independent.gov.uk/browne-report. Accessed August 2012.

Bryan, J. and Hayes, D. (eds) (2007) 'The McDonaldization of Further Education' in Hayes et al., *A Lecturer's Guide to Further Education*, Maidenhead: Open University Press.

Bynner, J. (2009) *Intervention and Disadvantage: A Life Course Approach*, NIACE Conference: Families, Learning Impact and the National Agenda, Sheffield 22 January 2009.

Bynner, J., McIntosh, S., Vignoles, A., Dearden, L., Reed, H. and Van Reenen, J. (2001) 'Improving Adult Basic Skills: Benefits to the Individual and to Society', *Research Report* No 251, London: Department for Education and Employment.

Bynner, J. and Parsons, S. (1998) *Use it or Lose it?* London: The Basic Skills Agency.

Cabinet Office (2011) *Opening Doors, Breaking Barriers: A Strategy for Social Mobility*, London: Cabinet Office.

Cara, O., Lister, J., Swain., J. and Vorhaus, J. (2010) *The Teachers Study*, London: National Research and Development Centre.

Coffield, F. (1997) *Can the UK Become a Learning Society?* The 4th Annual Education Lecture, Royal Society of Arts.

Coffield, F. (1999) 'Breaking the Consensus: Lifelong Learning as Social Control', *British Educational Research Journal*, Vol. 25, No. 4: 479–99.

Comings J. P., Parrella, A. and Soricone, L. (1999) 'Persistence among Adult Basic Education Students in Pre-GED Classes', *NCSALL Reports* #12, The National Center for the Study of Adult Learning and Literacy, Cambridge, MA: Harvard Graduate School of Education.

Committee on Higher Education (1963) *Higher Education: Report of the Committee Appointed by the Prime Minister under the Chairmanship of Lord Robbins 1961–63*, Cmnd. 2154, London: HMSO.

Cottle, V. (2011) 'Lifelong Learning' in Walkup, V., *Exploring Education Studies*, London: Pearson.

Crawley, J. (2005) *In at the Deep End: A Survival Guide for Teachers in Post Compulsory Education*, London: David Fulton Publishers.

Curzon, L. B. (ed.) (1990) *Teaching in Further Education*, 4th edition, London: Cassell.

DBIS (Department of Business Innovation and Skills) (2010a) *A Simplified FE Skills Funding System*, London: The Stationery Office.

DBIS (Department of Business Innovation and Skills) (2010b) *Skills for Sustainable Growth*, London: The Stationery Office.

DBIS (Department of Business Innovation and Skills) (2011a) *Making Prisons Work: Skills for Rehabilitation*, London: The Stationery Office.

DBIS (Department of Business Innovation and Skills) (2011b) *New Challenges, New Chances: Further Education and Skills System Reform Plan: Building a World Class Skills System*, London: The Stationery Office.

DBIS (Department of Business Innovation and Skills) (2012) *Community Learning Trust Pilots*, London: The Stationery Office.

Dearing Report (1997) National Committee of Inquiry into Higher Education Available from: http://www.ncl.ac.uk/ncihe/sumrep.htm. Accessed August 2012.

DES (Department for Education and Science) (1973) *Adult Education: A Plan for Development*, London: HMSO.

Dewey, J. (1916) *Democracy and Education*, New York: Free Press.

DfEE (Department for Education and Employment) (1998) *The Learning Age: A Renaissance for a New Britain*, London: The Stationery Office.

DfEE (Department for Education and Employment) (1999) *Improving Literacy and Numeracy: A Fresh Start*, The Report of the Working Group chaired by Sir Claus Moser, London: The Stationery Office.

DfEE (Department for Education and Employment) (2001a) *Skills for Life: The National Strategy for Improving Adult Literacy and Numeracy Skills*, London: The Stationery Office.

DfEE (Department for Education and Employment) (2001b) *Learning to Succeed: A Framework for Post-16 Learning*, London, The Stationery Office.

DfES (Department for Education and Skills) (2002a) *Success for All: Reforming Further Education and Training: Our Vision for the Future*, London: The Stationery Office.

DfES (Department for Education and Skills) (2002b) 'Evaluating Outcomes for Learners in Pathfinder Areas', *Research Report* 343, London: The Stationery Office.

DfES (Department for Education and Skills) (2002c) *Education and Skills: The Economic Benefit*, London: The Stationery Office.

DfES (Department for Education and Skills) (2002d) *Future of Higher Education*. Available from: www.dfes.gov.uk/highereducation/hestrategy/. Accessed August 2012.

DfES (Department for Education and Skills) (2003a) *21st Century Skills: Realising Our Potential*, London: The Stationery Office.

DfES (Department for Education and Skills) (2003b) *Skills for Life: The National Strategy for Improving Adult Literacy and Numeracy Skills, Focus on Delivery to 2007*, London: The Stationery Office.

DfES (Department for Education and Skills) (2003c) *The Skills for Life survey: A National Needs and Impact Survey of Literacy, Numeracy and ICT*, London: The Stationery Office.

DfES (Department for Education and Skills) (2003d) *21st Century Skills: Realising Our Potential; Individuals, Employers, Nation*, Norwich: The Licensing Division.

DfES (Department for Education and Skills) (2003e) *Widening Participation Strategy*, London: The Stationery Office.

DfES (Department for Education and Skills) (2004) *Equipping Our Teachers for the Future: Reforming Initial Teacher Training for the Learning and Skills Sector*, London; DfES, Standards Unit.

DfES (Department for Education and Skills) (2005) *Skills: Getting On in Business, Getting On at Work*, Cm 6483–11, London: The Stationery Office.

DfES (Department for Education and Skills) (2006) *Further Education: Raising Skills, Improving Life Chances*, London: The Stationery Office.

DIUS (Department for Innovation Universities and Skills) (2007) *World Class Skills: Implementing the Leitch Review of Skills in England*, London: The Stationery Office.

DIUS (Department for Innovation Universities and Skills) (2008) *The Learning Revolution White Paper*, London: The Stationery Office.

DIUS (Department for Innovation Universities and Skills) (2009) *Informal Adult Learning White Paper: The Learning Revolution*, London: The Stationery Office.

Dixon, L., Jones, E. and Southwood, S. (2011) *Boosting Capacity of Third Sector Organisations to Work with Young People Who are Not in Education, Employment or Training (NEET)*, Leicester: NIACE.

Drucker, P. F. (2003) *A Functioning Society: Selections from Sixty-five Years of Writing on Community, Society and Policy*, New Brunswick, NJ and London: Transaction Publishers.

Durkheim, E. (1982 [1895]) *The Rules of Sociological Method*, London: Macmillan.

DWP (Department for Work and Pensions) (2001) *Towards Full Employment in a Modern Society – United Kingdom, Third Report of the Low Pay Commission*. Available from: www.logos-net/ilo/150_base/en/init/uk_12.htm. Accessed August 2012.

DWP (Department for Work and Pensions) (2011) *The Work Programme*. Available from: www.dwp.gov.uk/policy/welfare-reform/the-work-programme/. Accessed August 2012.

Faure, E., Herrera, F., Kaddoura, A. R., Lopes, H., Petrovsky, A. V., Rahnema, M. and Ward, F. C. (1972) *Learning to Be: The World of Education Today and Tomorrow*, Paris: UNESCO.

Field, J. (2001) 'Lifelong Education', *International Journal of Lifelong Education*, Vo. 20, No. 1/2: 3–15.

Field, J. (2002) *Lifelong Learning and the New Educational Order*, Stoke-on-Trent: Trentham Books Limited.

Field, J. (2003) *Social Capital*, London: Routledge.

Field, J. (2005) *Social Capital and Lifelong Learning*, Bristol: Policy Press.

Field, J. (2008) *Social Capital*, 2nd edition, London: Routledge.

Finn, D. (2000) 'From Full Employment to Employability: A New Deal for Britain's Unemployed?' *International Journal of Manpower*, Vol. 21, No. 5: 384–99.

Foskett, N. H. and Hemsley-Brown, J. (2001) *Choosing Futures: Young People's Decision-making in Education, Training and Career Markets*, London: Routledge and Falmer Press.

Foster, A. (2005) *Realising the Potential: A Review of the Future Role of Further Education Colleges*, DfES, London: The Stationery Office.

Freire, P. (1996) *Pedagogy of the Oppressed* (20th anniversary edition), New York: Continuum.

Giddens, A. (2007) *Sociology*, 6th edition, London: Polity Press.

Gilbert, I. (2002) *Essential Motivation in the Classroom*, London: Routledge and Falmer Press.

Gray, F. (ed.) (2002) *Landscapes of Learning: Lifelong Learning in Rural Communities*, Leicester: NIACE.

Great Britain (1911) *National Insurance Act*, London: The Stationery Office.

Great Britain (1992) *Further and Higher Education Act*, London: The Stationery Office.

Great Britain (2009) *Apprenticeships, Skills, Children and Learning Act*, London: The Stationery Office.

HM Government (2005) *Reducing Re-offending through Skills and Employment*, London: The Stationery Office.

HM Government (2006) *Reducing Re-offending through Skills and Employment: Next Steps*, London: The Stationery Office.

HM Government (2010) *Building a Stronger Civil Society: a strategy for Voluntary and Community Groups, Charities and Social Enterprises*, London: The Stationery Office.

HM Government (2011) *Ending Gang and Youth Violence: A Cross-government Report including Further Evidence and Good Practice Case Studies*, London: The Stationery Office.

HM Government (2012) *Social Justice: Transforming Lives*, London: The Stationery Office.

Hodgson, A. and Spours, K. (1999) *New Labour's Educational Agenda*, London: Kogan Page.

Home Office (2007) *The Corston Report: A Report by Baroness Jean Corston of a Review of Women with Particular Vulnerabilities in the Criminal Justice System*, London: The Stationery Office.

Home Office (2010) *Drug Strategy 2010: Reducing Demand, Restricting Supply, Building Recovery: Supporting People to Live a Drug Free Life*, London: The Stationery Office.

Houle, C. (1964) *Continuing Your Education*, New York: McGraw-Hill.

House of Commons Library (2012) *Prison Population Statistics*, Available from: www.parliament. uk/briefing-papers/SN04334.pdf. Accessed August 2012.

Howard, U. (2009) *FE Colleges in a New Culture of Adult and Lifelong Learning: Inquiry into the Future of Lifelong Learning Sector Paper*, Leicester: NIACE.

Huitt, W. (2001) 'Motivation to Learn: An Overview', *Educational Psychology Interactive*, Valdosta, GA: Valdosta State University Available from: http://chiron.valdosta.edu/whuitt/col/ motivation/motivate.html. Accessed August 2012.

Illeris, K. (2003a) 'Adult Education as Experienced by the Learners', *International Journal of Lifelong Education*, Vol. 22, No. 1: 13–23.

Illeris, K. (2003b) 'Towards a Contemporary and Comprehensive Theory of Learning', *International Journal of Lifelong Education*, Vol. 22, No. 4: 396–406.

Illeris, K. (2004) *The Three Dimensions of Learning*, Leicester: National Institute of Adult Continuing Education.

Jarvis, P. (1987) *Adult Learning in the Social Context*, London: Croom Helm.

Jarvis, P. (1995) *Adult and Continuing Education*, 2nd edition, London: Routledge.

Jarvis, P. (2006) *From Adult Education to the Learning Society*, London: Routledge.

Jarvis, P. (2007) *Globalisation, Lifelong Learning and the Learning Society*, London: Routledge.

Jarvis, P. (ed.) (2011) *The Routledge International Handbook of Lifelong Learning*, London: Routledge.

Jenkins, R. (2002) *Pierre Bourdieu*, London: Routledge.

Kennedy, H. (1997) *Learning Works: Widening Participation in Further Education*, Coventry: Further Education Funding Council.

Kerka, S. (2000) *Lifelong Learning, Myths and Realities*, No. 9, Columbus, OH: ERIC Clearinghouse on Adult, Career and Vocational Education.

Knowles, M. S. (1975) *Self-directed Learning: A Guide for Learners and Teachers*, New York: Association Press.

Knowles, M. S., Holton III, E. F. and Swanson, R. A. (2005) *The Adult Learner*, London: Elsevier Butterworth Heinemann.

Labour Party (1995) *Labour Party Manifesto*, London: The Labour Party. Available from: www. labour.org.uk/manifesto. Accessed August 2012.

Larsen, K. and Istance, D. (2001) *Lifelong Learning for All*, Available from: www.oecdobserver.org/ news/archivestory.php/aid/432/Lifelong_learning_for_all.html. Accessed August 2012.

Lave, J. and Wenger, E. (1991) *Situated Learning: Legitimate Peripheral Participation*, Cambridge: Cambridge University Press.

Lee, W. O. (2007) 'Lifelong Learning in Asia: Eclectic Concepts, Rhetorical Ideals, and Missing Values. Implications from Values Education', paper presented at International Conference of Comparative Education, University of Hong Kong.

Lee, N. and Wright, J. (2011) *Off the Map? The Geography of NEETs*, Lancaster: Lancaster University, The Work Foundation.

Leitch, S. (2006) *Leitch Review of Skills: Prosperity for All in the Global Economy – World Class Skills*, London: The Stationery Office.

Levitas, R. (2005) *The Inclusive Society?* Hampshire: Palgrave MacMillan.

LLUK (Lifelong Learning UK) (2007) *Guidance for Awarding Institutions on Teacher Roles and Initial Teaching Qualifications*, London: LLUK.

Maginn, A. and Williams, M. (2002) *Institute for Employment Studies: An Assessment of Skill Needs in Post-16 Education and Training*, Nottingham: Department for Education and Skills.

McGivney, V. (1999) *Informal Learning in the Community: A Trigger for Change and Development*, Leicester: NIACE.

McNair, S. (2008) *Migration, Communities and Lifelong Learning*, Leicester: NIACE.

Merriam, S. and Caffarella, R. (1999) *Learning in Adulthood*, San Francisco: Jossey Bass.

MoJ (Ministry of Justice) (2007) *The Government's Response to the Report by Baroness Corston of a Review of Women with Particular Vulnerabilities in the Criminal Justice System*, London: The Stationery Office. Available from: http://www.official-documents.gov.uk/document/cm72/7261/7261.pdf. Accessed August 2012.

MoJ (Ministry of Justice) (2010) *Breaking the Cycle: Effective Punishment, Rehabilitation and Sentencing of Offenders*, London: The Stationery Office.

Moser, C. (1999) *A Fresh Start: Improving Literacy and Numeracy*, London: Department for Education and Employment.

NAS (National Apprenticeship Service) (online) Available from: www.apprenticeships.org.uk. Accessed August 2012.

National Association of Schoolmasters and Union of Women Teachers (2009) *Gangs and Schools*, Birmingham: NASUWT.

National Offender Management Service (online) Available from: www.justice.gov.uk/about/noms. Accessed August 2012.

NIACE (National Institute of Adult Continuing Education) (online) *Family Learning*, Leicester: NIACE. Available from: www.niace.org.uk. Accessed August 2012.

NTA (National Treatment Agency) (2009/10) National Treatment Agency for Substance Misuse, Available from: http://www.nta.nhs.uk/search.aspx?query=substance+abuse. Accessed August 2012.

OECD (Organisation for Economic Co-operation and Development) (online) Available from: http://www.oecd.org/. Accessed August 2012.

OECD (Organisation for Economic Co-operation and Development) (1973) *Recurrent Education: A Strategy for Lifelong Learning*, Paris: Organisation for Economic Co-operation and Development.

OECD (Organisation for Economic Co-operation and Development) (1996) *Lifelong Learning for All*, Paris: Organisation for Economic Co-operation and Development.

Offender and Learning Skills Service (2006) *The Offender's Learning Journey: Learning and Skills Provision for Adult Offenders in England*, Available from: www.bis.gov.uk/assets/biscore/corporate/migratedd/publications/o/olass_booklet.pdf. Accessed August 2012.

Office for Civil Society (2010) *Building a Stronger Civil Society: A Strategy for Voluntary and Community Groups, Charities and Social Enterprises*, London: The Stationery Office.

Ofsted (Office for Standards in Education) (2003) *The Initial Training of Further Education Teachers: A Survey*, London: Ofsted.

Ofsted (Office for Standards in Education) (2010) *Progress in Implementing Reforms in the Accreditation and Continuing Professional Development of Teachers in Further Education*, London: Ofsted.

O'Grady, A. (2008) 'Choosing to Learn or Chosen to Learn: A Qualitative Case Study of Skills for Life Learners', University of Nottingham: unpublished thesis.

O'Grady, A. (2009) 'Where Are We Now? An Exploration of the Provision of Teacher Training Programmes for the Learning and Skills Sector following the 2007 Workforce Reforms', unpublished, Leicester: NIACE.

Offender Learning and Skills Service (online) Available from: Skills Funding Agency, http://olass.skillsfundingagency.bis.gov.uk/. Accessed August 2012.

ONS (Office for National Statistics) (online) Office for National Statistics. Available at: www.ons.gov.uk/. Accessed August 2012.

Pahl, K. (2009) Interactions, Intersections and Improvisations: Studying the Multimodal Texts and Classroom Talk of Six to Seven Year Olds', *Journal of Early Childhood Literacy*, Vol. 9, No. 2: 188–210.

Parsons, S. and Bynner, J. (2002) *Basic Skills and Social Exclusion*, London: The Basic Skills Agency.

Parsons, T. (1961) *Theories of Society: Foundations of Modern Sociological Theory*, New York: Free Press.

Pateman, T. (2010) *Rural and Urban Areas: Comparing Lives Using Rural/Urban Classifications*, Regional Trends 43 210/11, London: Office of National Statistics.

Pintrich, P. R. and Schunk, D. H. (2002) *Motivation in Education: Theory, Research,* 2nd edition, New Jersey: Merrill Prentice Hall.

Putnam, R. D. (2000) *Bowling Alone: The Collapse and Revival of American Community*, New York: Simon & Schuster.

Rice, M. (1999) 'Dyslexia and Crime', *Prison Report*, 49: 18–19.

Rogers, A. (1992) *Adults Learning for Development*, London: Cassell.

Rogers, A. (2002) *Teaching Adults*, 3rd edition, Buckingham: Open University Press.

Rogers, A. (2003) *What is the Difference?* Leicester: NIACE.

Rogers, A. (2004) *Non-formal Education, Flexible Schooling or Participatory Education?* Hong Kong: Comparative Education Research Centre, University of Hong Kong.

Rodgers, G., Gore, C. and Figueiredo, J. B. (eds) (1995) 'United Nation Social Exclusion: Rhetoric', A Contribution to the World Summit for Social Development, Switzerland: ILO Publications.

Schuller, T. (2009) 'Crime and Lifelong Learning', *IFLL Thematic Paper* 5, Leicester: NIACE.

Schuller, T. and Watson, D. (2009) *Learning through Life Inquiry into the Future for Lifelong Learning*, Leicester: NIACE.

Sen, A. (2000) *Social Exclusion: Concept, Application, and Scrutiny*, Manila: Asian Development Bank.

Silver, H. (1994) 'Social Exclusion and Social Solidarity: Three Paradigms', *International Labour Review*, Vol. 133: 5–6.

Skills Funding Agency (online) Available from: http://skillsfundingagency.bis.gov.uk/. Accessed August 2012.

SEU (Social Exclusion Unit) (1997) *Social Exclusion Unit: Purpose, Work Priorities and Working Methods*, London: The Stationery Office.

Strategic Migration Partnership (online) Available from: www.emcouncils.gov.uk/Strategic-Migration-Partnership. Accessed August 2012.

Tough, A. (1967) *Learning Without a Teacher*, Toronto: Ontario Institute for Studies in Education.

UNESCO (United Nations Educational, Scientific and Cultural Organisation) (online) Available from: http://www.unesco.org Accessed August 2012.

United Nations (1995) *The Copenhagen Declaration and Programme of Action*, World Summit for Social Development, 6–12 March 1995, New York: United Nations Department of Publications.

Webb, J., Schirato, T. and Danaher, G. (2002) *Understanding Bourdieu*, Crows Nest, NSW: Allen and Unwin.

Webb, D. (2003) 'Employment and Training Programmes for the Unemployed', *Research Paper 03/13*, London: House of Commons Library, Available from: www.parliament.uk. Accessed August 2012.

Wenger, E. (1998) *Communities of Practice: Learning, Meaning and Identity*, New York: Cambridge University Press.

Wheeler, M., Smith, F. and Trayhorn, L. (1999) 'Mental Health and GPs and Adult Education Courses', cited in Hammond, C. and Feinstein L. (2006) 'The Effects of Adult Learning on Self-Efficacy', *London Review of Education*, Vol. 3, No. 3: 265–87.

WHO (World Health Organization) (1948) Adopted by the International Health Conference, New York, 19–22 June, 1946; signed on 22 July 1946 by the representatives of 61 States (Official Records of the World Health Organization, No. 2, p. 100) and entered into force on 7 April 1948.

Willis, P. (1977) *Learning to Labor: How Working Class Kids Get Working Class Jobs*, New York: Colombia University Press.

Wolf, A. (2002) *Does Education Matter? Myths about Education and Economic Growth*, London: Penguin.

Wolf, A. (2011) *Review of Vocational Education: The Wolf Report*, Available from: www.education.gov.uk/publications/eOrderingDownload/The%20Wolf%20Report.pdf. Accessed August 2012.

Wu, J. (2000) *Unemployment-related Benefits System in the United Kingdom*, Hong Kong: Legislative Council Secretariat.

Yeaxlee, B. A. (1929) *Lifelong Education*, London: Cassell.

Index